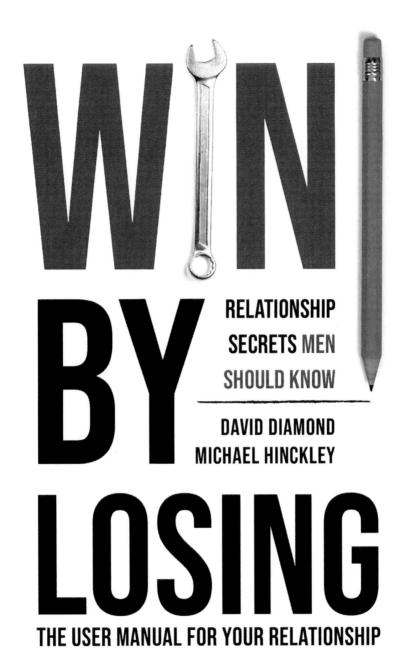

WIN

BY

RELATIONSHIP
SECRETS MEN
SHOULD KNOW

DAVID DIAMOND
MICHAEL HINCKLEY

LOSING

THE USER MANUAL FOR YOUR RELATIONSHIP

Paperback ISBN 978-1-99930-251-1

eBook ISBN 978-1-99930-250-4

Visit www.WinByLosingBook.com

Contact authors@WinByLosingBook.com

Facebook Page www.Facebook.com/WinByLosingBook

For our wives, Claire and Vera

PREFACE

David

After many years had passed it was good to see Michael again. There was so much to catch up: our lives had moved on, we both had families now, and we spent many hours exchanging our stories and experiences. Almost from nowhere we started talking about communication and relationships.

"Well," said Michael in his usual confident American way, "men should Win by Losing, you know what I mean?"

That was an ingenious way of bringing together so much of what we had been talking about. I knew exactly what he meant.

At that moment many different strands of ideas seemed to gel in new, interesting and exciting ways. After talking about this for the rest of the afternoon, Michael stopped, thought for a moment and proclaimed, "You know, we should write a book about this. It would make a real difference to people's lives."

The thought hadn't occurred to me. What an interesting idea. Could we really do it? Was there enough material for a book? It turned out there most certainly was plenty to write about.

Michael returned to America and we continued to develop our ideas through WhatsApp and Google Docs. It didn't take long for me to coin the term "Relationship Enabler," and for us to develop these ideas into chapters for our book. It's amazing how far we progressed by working in this way. We truly live in a creative age.

My degree in Psychology and my Master's degree in Applied Psychology, alongside what seemed like a lifetime of experience and a passion to contribute toward creating a better world, represented a good starting point. However, it turned out that writing a book was surprisingly difficult and took a considerable amount of time and determination. We were resolved to write in an inspiring and engaging manner, to include interactive sections for the reader to digest the material, and to present the material in a way that encouraged the reader to communicate more effectively. The result of all that hard work is this book.

I certainly hope this book makes a positive difference to the way you communicate with your partner. Intimate relationships are a double-edged sword: sure, everyone loves the passion—it's what makes the world go around—but it has the potential to bring with it so much unnecessary stress and unhappiness.

This book has been written to ensure you, and your partner, enjoy a happy and healthy relationship. It's been written *by* men *for* men. Of course, women are welcome to read it too, but it's written from a male perspective. So much of the media today is female-centric. In my view, there has been a determined effort to subtly shift the way men think toward a more female frame of mind. This, of course, hasn't worked. It has, however, left many men unsure of how to communicate effectively, especially in intimate relationships. One of my intentions behind writing this book was to put things right.

You don't need to be unhappy in your relationship to benefit from the ideas contained in this book. Nobody's perfect and there's always room for improvement. Being open to changing the way you communicate with your partner, to benefit from what you are about to read, is a prerequisite. Those changes don't necessarily have to be major; small changes really can, and do, make a big difference.

Sure, a few may find some of the material familiar and you'll only benefit from nuggets of ideas you hadn't considered before. Most men, however, will find this book to be a treasure trove of ideas laid out in a clear and action-oriented way. Let's face it, if the book doesn't inspire you to do something differently, there isn't much point in reading it.

All men (and possibly women too) who read this book will take something meaningful away with them to put into practice; something which will improve or even transform the way they communicate with their partners.

Changes to the way you communicate with your partner really will yield significant results.

DAVID DIAMOND
MARCH 31, 2019

Michael

As David, my good friend from my post-college days in England, has said, there is really something for every man in this book. We met up at a hotel adjoining an airport terminal at London Heathrow. As it happens, that was serendipitous because there was something like a two-mile covered walkway from the hotel to the airport terminal. I had also only had a few hours of sleep due to an overnight international flight, so the walk was great to get things moving. We spent probably three to four hours walking continuously, talking about our lives initially, after which we landed upon the most important topic; namely, how much there is that we have learned and observed about the intimate relationships between men and women, and how much men don't understand about how to find their "happiness" in that type of relationship.

I remember when I first learned Karate in college and was confused when I saw people with different black-belt rankings. I asked my instructor how one person, who appeared to be technically much stronger and faster than another, could be ranked lower. My instructor replied that the person who had the higher ranking was measured by how hard they had worked to reach their ultimate potential given their physical and mental abilities. He went on to say that although the lower-ranking student had much better technique, they had not worked hard to realize their individual potential and thus did not merit a higher ranking.

This is a difficult concept for Western men to grasp, and in much the same way, part of understanding "Win by Losing" is to look at ourselves and ask what we want in our relationship with a woman, and what is important, rather than compare ourselves to other couples who look like they "have it all." When we do that, we will realize that Win by Losing can give us the tools to improve our relationships. We are not interested in, and should not compare our relationships to anyone else's, because each person has their own individual journey and as part of a couple. The couple that appears to have it all may not have it all, so look at your own relationship and make it better!

It is our hope that you take the principles in this book to heart and learn that you can reduce stress, conflict, and angst, while at the same time, work toward a more fulfilling relationship that can impact all areas of your life positively. Just like anyone starting on a diet does not lose all the weight overnight, this is a lifestyle change, and sticking with it day in day out, will yield the results you seek.

I wish you all the greatest of joy and look forward to hearing from you.

On your marks … get set … go Win by Losing!

MICHAEL HINCKLEY
MARCH 31, 2019

CONTENTS

PRELUDE:
Same challenges, different solutions

If you are in a relationship, consider these questions:

- Do you wonder what happened to the passionate person you fell in love with?

- Is there never enough time to do the things which are important to you?

- Do you find yourself in heated arguments with your partner about the same things?

If you are single, consider these questions:

- Do you wonder why your previous relationships have been so difficult?

- Did you find previous partners to be unpredictable and difficult to understand?

- Do you want a happier and healthier relationship next time?

If you have answered 'yes' to any of these questions, then this book is for you.

Win by Losing will teach you a method to distinguish between which arguments to fight and what battles are not worth the effort. You will learn how to communicate in a healthier way and avoid endless arguments and negativity. Our approach will enable you to address the issues and transform your relationship.

Read on for examples of how various approaches to relationships can lead to different outcomes.

Fred

Fred was a winner. Highly competitive and extremely bright, he won at everything he did. At school he won all the school prizes: Whether sports, academic subjects, or extracurricular activities, he was brilliant at everything he did. From an early age, he had learned that being right worked for him. Every time his class teacher asked a question, his hand would be the first to shoot into the air and he would be rewarded with a, "Well done, Fred" from his teacher for knowing the right answer.

When Fred started work he was quickly rewarded for being right, either through a promotion or big salary increases. When Fred started his own business, in a short period of time it grew into a large successful enterprise. As he was well-educated, driven, and right most of the time, this proved to be an unstoppable combination in his business endeavors. Within a few years Fred became a successful and wealthy businessman.

However, what had worked so well at school, university, and in business didn't work so well in relationships. It was implicit in Fred's personality to win and everything had to be *his* way. It was Fred's way or no way. He never gave in and never allowed anyone to change his mind.

Fred's good looks and charismatic personality attracted the girls but, for one reason or another which he could never quite understand, they didn't stay for long. Wealth certainly helped, and with money came some very pretty girlfriends, one of whom he married in a suitably extravagant wedding. But however expensive his wedding, it turned out to be far cheaper than his divorce.

Driving home from work one day, he started to really think about his life and what he had achieved. Now in middle age, he lived alone and saw his children every other weekend. He had more money than he knew what to do with, but was lonely and unhappy. This was not the life he had expected. How had it all gone so wrong?

Jane and Peter

Jane and Peter had just got engaged and were renting their first apartment together. It was relatively small, but met their needs. One Saturday morning they left home early and went to a large out-of-town shopping center. It was a day they had set aside from their busy lives to choose the furniture for their new apartment. They stopped off for a quick coffee before entering their first department store.

Jane announced she loved brightly colored cushions and wanted to ensure they matched the throw, which she had planned to purchase later that day. She had seen both in a magazine and produced the piece of paper she had carefully removed from the magazine, to ensure they bought something similar. Peter had no interest in cushions and didn't like throws. This was not the type of look which appealed to him. He wasn't impressed by the thought of bright colors either. He had lived on his own before meeting Jane and had avoided bright colors intentionally. Peter's ego told him *he* knew best. All he needed to do was to disagree with Jane and he would get his way. There weren't going to be any brightly colored fabrics in his apartment, and definitely no throws or cushions.

It's fair to say the ensuing argument lasted a very long time. It spoiled the rest of the day—and the memory of this particularly important day and what should have been a special shopping outing together. Peter would not have it any other way: He had to win and therefore stuck to his guns. Perhaps unsurprisingly, they didn't buy anything that day and not a word was spoken in the car on their way home.

Life carried on for the young couple and the argument eventually passed, as arguments do. Several months later Jane and Peter moved into their new apartment. In celebration of this achievement, they invited their best friends over. Andrew was Peter's best friend and Jane had known

Susan since high school. It was a great match and the four of them thoroughly enjoyed each other's company. Jane was keen to show off her new furniture and took them straight into the lounge.

"How lovely!" Susan exclaimed, genuinely happy to see Jane looking so pleased with herself.

"Oh yes," said Jane. "I especially like the way our cushions and throw match so well. Those bright colors really complement each other."

Ryan

Ryan had a good career with a lot of responsibility at work. He made important decisions and the company valued him. At home, Ryan let his wife make all the decisions which he knew were important to her. She wanted to change the color of the kitchen walls to blue, and although not his preferred color, it was fine by him. She decided to have a pet and wanted a dog: He wasn't a dog person but, no matter, they got a dog. She wanted to go on a beach holiday—they had a beach holiday. She wanted to go out for a pizza one evening—pizza it was.

Ryan met with his friends every Wednesday (they'd been doing this for years). When they first met this was for drinks, then it evolved into squash, which eventually became football and then drinks again. Over the years, Ryan's partner Jenny occasionally made arrangements on a Wednesday, expecting Ryan to change his arrangements too. This never happened as he consistently stuck to his guns. Wednesday was his night out and he would not allow any exceptions. He knew instinctively a firm, consistent approach was needed. He didn't mind *losing* where everything else was concerned, as he didn't particularly care, but Wednesday nights were something different and important to him. Jenny knew this and, despite occasionally attempting to navigate around this, accepted it. They had a long and happy marriage. He was the boss at work and she, for the most part, was in charge at home. It worked for both of them; they were happy together.

Over the years, Ryan watched as some of his closest friends battled their way through their marriages followed by multiple failed relationships, becoming poorer each time they changed partners: Poorer through the cost of divorce and/or through the heavy emotional price paid as a consequence of the breakups and divorce. He watched as they ended up miserable, angry, and alone. Ryan often wondered why they didn't just let their partners have their own way without an argument or series of arguments. Somehow, their partners got their way in the end anyway, so why did they choose to argue their way from beginning to end? He wondered what these men were gaining by adopting this fateful approach.

Jim

Jim was someone who was pretty laid-back, and most of the time he preferred to avoid arguments and valued peace above being right or having the last word. Of course, Jim had his moments at work and with certain family members—he was no doormat—but this was not his preferred way of dealing with life's challenges. Most of his friends would say he was gentle, unassuming and easy-going. He had the type of personality that meant he was relaxed most of the time, and liked having peace of mind and time to enjoy his life.

Unlike some of his friends, Jim did not chase success or advancement in the traditional male sense, nor did he want to dominate or have everyone listen to him all the time, telling him how great he was. He said what needed to be said, but did so in what most people interpreted as a friendly and direct way.

Rather than love the sound of his own voice, Jim didn't always have much to say, but listened a lot and was generally very complimentary and positive when he did speak. He valued discussion and differing points of view much more than he valued forcing people to agree with him. In short, he was the polar opposite of Fred (see above). Jim had just passed the twenty-year mark in his marriage and, while it was no bed of roses, it worked and he was happy.

He achieved this by generally not fighting battles which he knew he would lose and were, in fact, unimportant in the bigger picture. Jim knew what he wanted from his relationship and just focused on those things. He allowed things to go the way they were destined to go in the end and was wise in knowing the outcome at the beginning—unlike Fred and Peter, who assumed they would win and had to control every minor to major decision because they knew best.

If Jim had been with his wife at the furniture store it would have gone something like this:

"Honey, I know you were talking about going to the furniture store this weekend. Did you have a chance to think about which shop you want to go to and what type of cushions and throws you think would be best for the couch? You usually have a really good sense of these things."

Partner: "Yes, I'm really pleased you remembered. We should go to FGH Furniture. I already looked it up online, so I know what I want, but I want to see things in person to confirm."

(*At the store*) Partner: "What do you think of these?"

Jim took a look at the brightly colored cushions and had to admit to himself that they would not be his first choice. However, he had the insight and foresight to know where this conversation was heading and said, "Oh, those are lovely. Do you like the color and the feel?"

To which his partner replied, "Yes, I think these are perfect. I'm glad you agree. We really made the right choice."

"Yes," Jim replied smiling at his partner, "we did."

Looking at these examples, Ryan and Jim communicated in a way which enabled them to have happy and fulfilling relationships with their partners. Throughout this book we will explain how you too can achieve this positive outcome using the Win by Losing Method.

What's Next?

In the next chapter we will introduce you to the Win by Losing Method.

PART I

What Win by Losing is About

CHAPTER 1
Introduction

If you always do what you've always done, you'll always get
what you've always got.

HENRY FORD, FOUNDER OF THE FORD MOTOR COMPANY

Why read this chapter? What's in it for you?

In this chapter we will cover:

- ► What it's all about: What we mean by Win by Losing;
- ► Context: Why it's so important where Win by Losing is concerned;
- ► Single? A Fresh Start;
- ► The fast pace of change: Society has changed and relationships too;
- ► A way of life: Why Win by Losing is a lifestyle choice;
- ► Key Points;
- ► Questions and Answers;
- ► Multiple Choice;
- ► Take Action;
- ► What's Next?

An explanation: What Is Win By Losing?

Stop for a moment.

We all have busy lives but, right now, we need to you stop.

That's right. just **stop** and **think**.

What do you want from your intimate relationship? What makes you happy?

- Companionship?

- Intimacy?

- Friendship?

- Family?

- Freedom?

- Some peace and quiet?

- Time to pursue interests and hobbies?

- Time for your friends?

What is it that makes you happy in your relationship? Is it only one of the above, or possibly, and more likely, a combination?

Don't just read this list and move on to the next paragraph; give yourself five minutes to consider what it is that you want from your relationship. It doesn't matter if you aren't in a relationship right now as it's still a valid set of questions. You may have never stopped to think about this before. **Now is your opportunity**.

Whatever it is, whatever will ensure your long-term happiness with your partner, you can be sure of one thing; you are far more likely to achieve them by communicating in a more effective way. Effective communication underlines everything in an intimate relationship, as does having an appreciation of how your partner thinks. There is a way to ensure better outcomes with fewer arguments and happier times together. That way is called **Win by Losing**.

Win by Losing is a way to handle your intimate relationship that focuses on knowing when to choose your battles and having a better understanding how to communicate effectively with the woman in your life. This enables both you and your partner to have a happy, meaningful and satisfying relationship.

This can be achieved by:

- Understanding what you want and hold dear in your relationship;
- Discussing and understanding how to solve problems together;
- Recognizing the cost of arguments and doing something about it;
- Developing constructive direct communication;
- Making sure that what you hear is what she said;
- Identifying how to react in unfamiliar situations.

It's a simple way of communicating which works in conjunction with the following five Relationship Enablers:

1. **I won't back down: Enforce your Ground Rules** (Chapter 4): Ground Rules are the most important things to you in your life and relationship. Enforcing them ensures they stay in place.

2. **Make every conversation matter: Listening with Intent** (Chapter 5): A way of listening to your partner which encourages effective communication.

3. **We're in this together: Common Purpose** (Chapter 6): Understanding why you are in a relationship together to ensure you both achieve the outcomes you desire.

4. **Just accept it: Acceptance of what we can and cannot change** (Chapter 7): No matter how much you love your partner, you can't change her. Change can only come from within you.

5. **Say what you mean: Straight Talking** (Chapter 8): Saying what's really on your mind in a calm and constructive manner.

This way of communicating costs nothing to put in place and yet can genuinely transform your relationship. All the tools you need are explained clearly throughout this book in an action-oriented way. This book applies to men who face typical relationship issues with their Western female partners, and transcends class, career, ethnicity, religion, and economic status.

Layout matters: How we have formatted this book

Every chapter of this book follows the same format:

- Outline of what will be covered per chapter;

- Main chapter content;

- A summary of the chapter's key points;

- Questions and answers, to aid understanding;

- Multiple choice questions (with answers available in Appendix 2);

- Take action section, for you to apply the content of that chapter in the context of either your *current* or, if you are single, your *next* relationship;

- A 'What's next' section which briefly tells you what we will cover in the next chapter.

Two ways of reading: Active vs. Passive

It's not enough to just read this book; you need to act. We encourage you to read *actively*. If you really want to experience a genuine transformation in your intimate relationship, then you need to read actively and apply the "Take Action" sections at the end of each chapter to the way you communicate with your partner. Alternatively, "Appendix 1: Your 90-Day Action Plan" contains the questions and action points from all of the "Take Action" sections in an accessible format.

How you intend to approach this book is, of course, entirely up to you. However, we are keen to improve as many relationships as we can, and would like yours to be one of them. Please read actively, you will get so much more out of this book. It may surprise you.

Where intimate relationships are concerned, although arguably a generalization, in our view most men just want a stress-free, loving, intimate relationship with their partner. Essentially, by reading this book in an active manner and following up on the *Take Action* sections at the end of every chapter, your current relationship—or, if you are single, your next relationship—is far more likely to be happier for you and your partner.

This book won't make you more intelligent, gifted, or charismatic. However, what it will do is to provide you with a set of actionable techniques and the depth of understanding needed to have a happy and satisfying relationship with a modern independent woman.

It's about you: Your circumstances

There is no *best time* to read this book. You could be in a happy relationship and are open to suggestions as to how to make it even better; your relationship could be a nightmare and you are searching for ways to make it better (perhaps somehow reset it to the way it was when you first met); you might have just been through a messy breakup and want to ensure that doesn't happen again; or you may be single and enjoying the freedom that provides. Whatever your circumstances, there is plenty of material in this book which you will find relevant, insightful, and useful.

Single? Time for a fresh start?

If you're single you can;

1. Stay single;

2. Be a professional bachelor; or

3. Look for that special someone.

The first choice is infinitely preferable to being trapped and unhappy in a destructive relationship. There is, of course, nothing wrong with remaining single and many people decide that's the preferred option for them.

Being a professional bachelor, the second option, may be fun for a while but is unlikely to bring long-term happiness. Like a child in a candy store, many think the next chocolate will be even better than the last. There'll always be someone around the corner who's younger, prettier, has a better figure, has more money, or less emotional baggage. If you see your partner in the same way as a smartphone or car that always needs upgrading to the latest model, then this book is not for you. We are focused on a long-term intimate relationship with one woman.

The third option of finding that special someone is tough. It's always been tough but now it seems to be tougher than ever—we have social media and apps to thank for that. The creation of perfect images has somehow led to the illusion of the perfect personality too. It's human nature, after all, to judge a book by its cover. The truth is that nobody is perfect. More than anything else, the way you communicate with the people you meet will determine your level of perceived compatibility and whether you are able to forge a happy life together.

What really underlies a happy long-term relationship? It's not about romantic love. We can slip in and out of romantic love far too easily for that to be the case. It's not about marriage either. Gone are the days when marriage as an institution kept two people together.

So, if it's not about romantic love or marriage, what the secret to long-term happiness? It's having a *loving friendship*. Genuine loving friendship with your partner forms the solid basis for a happy long-lasting relationship. An integral part of loving friendship is trust and respect – who can be close friends with someone they don't trust and respect? You can't have one without the other and that's what makes loving friendship so important in relationships.

Money may pay the bills and let you take nice holidays, but communicating in an understanding and effective way will enable you to have a happy relationship.

Although this book has been written from the perspective of the reader being in a current relationship, the material is equally valid, useful, and applicable to you if you're not.

Open to interpretation: Intimacy and you

We mention "intimacy" throughout this book. Whether that means **quality time** talking together, going for a walk in the park, holding hands, having a cuddle, kissing or more, is up to you and your partner.

How you choose to interpret the term "intimacy" will work equally well when you take the ideas contained in this book and apply them to your relationship.

Why is this? It's because Win by Losing is a lifestyle choice rather than a therapeutic intervention. It applies to countless situations and contexts where intimate relationships are concerned. Our approach considers the way men and women think. It has taken many years to develop, will transform your understanding of your partner, and has the potential to fundamentally change the way you communicate together.

You will notice there aren't specific chapters to help you tackle specific issues such as, "How to argue less," "How to stop being nagged," or "How to ensure you have more time to yourself/with your friends." These problem areas are addressed in the book by adopting the **Win by Losing** method and communicating in a way which is consistent with the five **Relationship Enablers**. Adopt this approach and all these issues, and a lot more besides, will either melt away or become far easier to handle. The extent to which this happens will be mainly down to how you and your partner recognize the need to improve your relationship and adopt our simple approach.

Fresh start: Doing things differently

As Henry Ford's epigraph at the start of this chapter asserts, "If you always do what you have always done, you will always get what you always got."

This statement accurately captures much about the way we all behave and, in our case, how we all communicate. We quickly establish routines and familiar patterns at work, with friends, and in our intimate relationships. This book is about learning to do things differently where intimate relationships are concerned. Whereas it's written from a man's perspective, and will therefore be most effective for men, the authors anticipate that women will also find the content useful. It will provide them with a fresh perspective about why men behave in the way that they do. Although we are all individuals, with our own experiences, values, beliefs and perspectives on life, there is, in fact, much which all men and all women have in common.

Context: Why it matters

Everyone knows what the word "beautiful" means. However, a change in context will change the meaning of the word. Take this joke, for example:

Teacher: Good morning, class. Today we are going to talk about the word "beautiful." Can anyone give me a sentence with the word "beautiful" in it, not once but twice?

Girl: Yes, miss. It was a *beautiful* sunny morning and I went outside to watch the *beautiful* butterflies in my garden.

Teacher: Well done. That was a lovely example.

Johnny: I have an example too, miss.

Teacher: Wonderful. Let's hear your example, Johnny.

Johnny: This morning, when we were having breakfast my fifteen-year-old sister told my dad she was pregnant. He almost choked on his breakfast before looking up from his bowl of cereal and exclaimed, "What? You're pregnant? Oh, that's *beautiful*, just f****** *beautiful*."

In many ways context is everything. It defines the meaning for all that follows.

If you have ever been to a rock concert, you will know that it can be hot, loud, and crammed full of people. The same can be said of any city's mass transportation system. We doubt you would say rush hour on the London Underground or the New York City Subway is enjoyable. In fact, pop concerts are louder, more cramped, and even hotter than morning trips to work, yet people love pop concerts and will pay much more than a subway ticket for the experience. The difference between the two is their context: Watching and listening to your favorite band perform live is a completely different context from traveling to work, and therefore we experience them differently. **Context is everything.**

We cannot overemphasize the importance of context. The meaning of what we say is dependent upon the context within which it is said.

Context in action: Point of view

In 1986, a well-known newspaper in the United Kingdom, *The Guardian*, ran a television advertisement now referred to as the "Point of View." It provided an excellent way of understanding the importance of context as it demonstrated brilliantly how meaning is determined by context. If you can, take a minute now to watch the advertisement on YouTube. https:// www.youtube.com/watch?v=_SsccRkLLzU

Now that you have seen the advertisement, you will appreciate how the behavior of the main character is determined not by what he is doing, but by the wider context within which his behavior takes place. An understanding of what he is doing and why he behaves that way takes on a completely different meaning when we see an alternative perspective and the wider environment.

Only at the end of the advertisement do we understand that the behavior of the young man running into an older man was not to attack him, but to save him from imminent and mortal danger.

Context: There's a first time for everything

The middle-aged man lay quietly, waiting for her to arrive. Slightly nervous, as he had never done something like this before, he couldn't help but notice the sweet scent in the air and soft hum of the air-conditioning in the small room. He continued to wait. He found the combination of the scent and warmth of the room relaxing and the worries of his day seemed to melt away. Was this the right thing to do? It seemed quite expensive, but he had no frame of reference where cost was concerned. Perhaps she was overcharging him. It was difficult to tell and too late to back out now.

Eventually, the silence was broken by a young lady entering the room. The time had finally come.

What's happening here? Probably not what *you* had in mind right now! Perhaps if we provided some context it might become clearer. Our middle-aged man recently hurt his back and his family doctor recommended a physiotherapist. He didn't want to go ahead with this treatment but his partner insisted. She knew of an excellent physiotherapist who had treated her brother for a similar issue. The meaning—**what's actually happening here**—really is dependent on the context, and that context turned out to be different from the mental image you were probably developing in your mind.

Our context: Win by Losing

With all this in mind, it's important to appreciate the context of this book. This book has one context and one context alone: intimate relationships between a man and a woman who are not blood relatives. In this book, we are *only* concerned with intimate relationships, nothing else.

Please don't apply our ideas, for example, to your parents or siblings. The outcomes would be unpredictable as the dynamics in those types of relationships are completely different from those in intimate relationships. Don't apply the ideas to your place of work, as that's also a different context. If you are in the middle of negotiating a complex business deal or a salary increase, we very much doubt you will Win by Losing. Don't think these ideas will work when complaining about a poor product or service. They won't.

Win by Losing has been written to address the many common challenges men encounter on a day-to-day basis with their intimate partners, when the partners in question are women.

Understanding the book's content, and acting on it, will lead to happier intimate relationships. This, in turn, will make both of your lives happier and more fulfilling. If you attempt to apply these ideas in any other context, just know you are taking an informed risk which may not go to plan and may go badly for you. You have been warned.

That said, by reading this book you will learn the method of Win by Losing. You will learn from genuine situations that real people face. You will realize the inevitable futility of appearing to win and needing to be in control where your partner is concerned. You will also learn a lot about yourself, as a man, and about the way women think (from a man's perspective).

We bet you have heard the saying "It's a man's world." In many ways we are changing that to "It's a world for you both when it comes to having a happy intimate relationship."

If you always want to get your own way, if you don't want to focus on, and work at, developing a happy relationship, if you can't deal with someone disagreeing with your view, or want your partner to always give you an easy time, then get a Cavalier King Charles Spaniel and give this book to someone else. If you want a happy and long-lasting relationship with a modern, dynamic, and independent Western woman then keep reading!

Win by Losing: A lifestyle choice

We should point out that this book is not an alternative to professional counseling. If your relationship is in trouble, there's a lot at stake (house, money, kids, career, etc.) and if you were about to reach out for professional help, then that's what you should do. This book is not a substitute for counseling or any other type of professional help.

This book is a lifestyle choice, it is a way to live your life where your intimate relationship is concerned.

Too often relationships don't work out as planned and the cause remains a puzzle. This book unlocks that puzzle by showing you how to communicate with your partner in a better and more effective way, leading to the type of behavior you, as a man, want to experience with your partner.

Nothing stays the same: A changing society

It has become a truism to say we live in times of great change. We won't dwell on this increasingly hectic pace of change, other than to say that change is the new norm, and that also includes the way relationships work. The dynamics between men and women have changed drastically, especially in the past sixty years.

There is no escaping the fact that we are all a product of the society within which we live, and society has changed more since the 1960s than in the preceding 2,000 years. This has impacted the way we communicate with each other in every aspect of our lives.

We are not simply referring to the invention of the contraceptive pill, smartphones, social media, etc. Consider the way men and women interact today (this includes our body language; what we say; the amount of time we spend together; how we spend our time together; and how we communicate when we are apart), compared to how we interacted in Victorian times, which were less than 200 years ago. It's completely different.

Change is all around us and affects every part of our lives.

This is not necessarily a bad thing. In fact, change has brought great benefits to our lives. Who can imagine being able to function at home or at work without using a computer, tablet, or smartphone? We are all used to having a smartphone pretty much attached to us and it's difficult to understand how anyone got anything done before they were invented. We can't imagine making weekend arrangements, exchanging information or keeping in touch with our partners, friends and family without one.

The contraceptive pill: Once invented, it changed the world

Equally important in terms of new technology is the invention of the contraceptive pill, which arguably did more to transform the lives of women than any other invention. The ability to choose when or whether to have children changed the power dynamics between men and women fundamentally, as it enabled women to build their own businesses or develop their careers in a way which was infinitely more difficult without the pill. Of course, there are other forms of contraception, but it was the pill which ultimately changed society's view of a woman's role, both at work and in the home.

Women are no longer destined to have children and look after the home as was the case for thousands of years. Their role in society, and what is expected from the modern woman, have altered drastically, and continue to evolve. The inevitable result is a corresponding change in dynamics between men and women.

The power balance has shifted in the woman's favor and men need to learn how to communicate differently, in order to achieve success in their relationships.

The idea that the main reason a Western woman finds a husband is to find a provider/protector is no longer true. It is often a voluntary choice based on other higher-level areas of common interest that provide the reason for a couple being together. Even the existence of adoption and fertility clinics allows a woman to choose to be a single parent and forego meeting a man for economic or reproductive reasons.

*What then is a man to do? Adopt the **Win by Losing Method.** Read on to learn more about it.*

Setting Western women free: Evolution of divorce laws and ability to vote

As important as the pill was, the evolution of divorce laws, and the concept of no fault–no shame divorce allowed Western women—who had traditionally needed permission, or a fault-evidence-based reason to be approved for divorce—to be set free from a destructive relationship without relying on a man's permission.

Fighting for, and gaining, the right to vote was another important social change for women that foreshadowed the pill, divorce modernization, as well as greater and fairer representation in the workforce (although there is still a long way to go in this area), which heralded a fundamental shift in women's traditional roles. These changes eroded the economic imperative for staying married, as a result of women being dependent on their husbands' income, and removed the fear of destitution should they divorce. Today, quite rightly, we all have a choice.

A limited understanding: Men's understanding of women

Most men don't understand women at all. They rely partly on mass media, but mostly on unmentioned behaviors passed down through generations. Anyone who has brought up children will know how very young children absorb everything around them: they learn effortlessly without being aware that they are doing so. Their ability, for example, to learn new words and use them quickly in the correct context, just by listening to what is being said around them, is truly astonishing. Their capacity for learning does not stop at what is being said or explained to them; it includes *all* the behaviors they see and hear around them.

Adults therefore can't help but teach children unspoken social skills, and thus demonstrate what children quickly interpret as the *right* way to communicate. This includes how to interact with men and women and has a direct impact on the type of relationships they will form as adults, whether with good friends, work colleagues, family, or in their intimate relationships.

The typical male understanding of how to behave toward women has been around for a long time. It originated long before the Internet existed, before the invention of the contraceptive pill, before central heating, before the First and Second World Wars, even before every home had electricity and running hot and cold water.

It's based on a set of extremely old values, social norms, behaviors, and beliefs, which were essential to daily survival in a hostile pre-modern world. Those are completely out of sync with the modern Western world we live in today. Together, these powerful forces combine to have a direct (and normally unconscious) impact on the way we deal with issues that we encounter in life, including how men communicate with women. However, they were developed originally to handle a different type of woman from a bygone age. She might still exist in some corners of the Western world but generally speaking, the type of woman you will meet or have as a partner is "modern" by all measures of the term.

The *old-fashioned* woman, for whom the values, social norms, behaviors, and beliefs were designed—with her reliance on a man, an inability to fend for herself, no access to contraception or a career, and her primary purpose based on serving her man, making sure his dinner was ready for him, and so on—has disappeared in the Western world for good. From your point of view, whether this is a good or bad development is irrelevant. In many cases, the typical man's hormonal and social evolution has not adapted in relationships and society to the rapid social and technological changes in women's roles. This therefore predisposes men to handle relationship challenges in clumsy and ineffective ways.

Generally, what men learn as babies and as they grow up about how to communicate in intimate relationships, does not serve them well when applied to modern, free-thinking, independent Western women.

When the intuitive approach is ineffective: Win by winning

What approach do men normally adopt when communicating with their partners? There are many, but we will consider just one: Men, generally speaking, are competitive and want to win. They *Win by Winning*. This means that, if there is a difference of opinion, they want to win at any cost. It doesn't matter if this is at work, with friends, or with their partners. They want to walk away knowing they were right so they can "feel like a man".

Unsure if this applies to you? Stop for a moment and think about when you had a difference of opinion with someone. It doesn't matter who or when. How did that work out for you? Were you right? How did it feel? What were the consequences of your actions?

If you were right, the chances are it felt good. If you were wrong, and accepted this to be the case, how did that feel? Men don't like to be wrong—neither, for that matter, do women—as being wrong doesn't feel great. When you were wrong you felt weak, like a loser and not "like a man". Our egos tell us we are always right, and that's what normally drives our behavior.

When we get something wrong our egos take a hit which never goes down well. After the event, the typical ego will analyze the events that culminated in the failure and convince itself that it was right all along. You have experienced this—we all have.

Men have grown up in an environment which has taught them that they need to win, and they do that by wanting to win in every context, so they can feel "like a man".

Quite rightly, parents encourage this ego and reward their children for being right. At a very early age we learn that being right leads to praise, and getting something wrong leads to being corrected or chastised. In some cases, being wrong can lead to physical pain. Failing to follow instructions is often the result of our ego telling us something different from the person giving the instruction.

"Don't touch the stove. It's very hot." The child's ego—they develop one from a very early age—disagrees and thinks it knows best. "What does Mommy know about that? Touch the stove, it'll be fine."

Whose voice has the greatest impact on the child's behavior and what does this lead to? That's right: A burned hand and lots of tears.

Children and adults alike are immensely forgiving of their egos and will happily listen to them in the future, no matter how badly things turn out. This applies to everyone—including you.

In most circumstances wanting to win is no bad thing: It drives innovation, builds companies, creates wealth for the owners and jobs for everyone else. The great innovators and leaders of our time wouldn't have existed without the drive for success and believing in themselves; believing they were right. Steve Jobs certainly seemed to have had an ego and a half. He knew he was right and wouldn't let anyone get in his way. He won by winning and, in doing so, created and grew one of the most successful companies on the planet.

These types of behaviors are reinforced, for example, in sport and are a direct consequence of the daily survival skills that were needed by our cave ancestors. Unfortunately, those types of behaviors are not effective or, in many ways appropriate, in modern intimate relationships with women. One tool, method, or approach does not work in every scenario.

In life, wanting to win is no bad thing.

The context where the belief in "Win by Winning" can be destructive is where it's applied to modern intimate relationships. We use the term "modern" to emphasize the here and now—the Modern Age with a relatively new dynamic between men and women in the Western world—where both rightly have the potential and opportunity to be just as successful and independent as each other. This relatively new dynamic is why most men will have far happier relationships by adopting the Win by Losing method.

Key Points

1. Society has changed and Win by Winning is no longer an effective approach when communicating with a modern, independent Western woman.

2. The better you communicate with your partner, the more likely you will have a happy relationship.

3. This book only applies to intimate relationships between a man and a woman.

4. This book will only improve the way you communicate with your partner when you *take action*. Please read in an *active* rather than a passive way.

5. Whether or not you are in a relationship, this book contains relevant, insightful, and useful material for you.

6. "Intimacy" means whatever you want it to mean: having a close conversation, holding hands, having a cuddle, kissing, or more.

7. Win by Losing is a lifestyle choice. It's a way of living your life from now on.

Questions and Answers

Q: I've just ended a difficult relationship. Does this book apply to me?

A: Yes. No matter what your circumstances are, this book contains plenty of information you will find useful and will help you in your next relationship. It will help you to better understand mistakes made in the last relationship you had.

Q: What's the difference between active and passive reading?

A: Passive reading is reading a book but *not taking any action*. Active reading is *taking action* and, where necessary, changing the way you communicate with your partner.

Q: What do you mean by "intimacy"?

A: In Win by Losing, it means the level of intimacy that is right for you and your partner.

Q: If Win by Losing works for intimate relationships, will it work in other areas of life?

A: No!

Q: Win by Winning works for me at work, so why won't it work with my partner?

A: In life, there's nothing wrong with wanting to win. However, where intimate relationships are concerned, it doesn't work that way. The context is different.

Q: Where's the section on how to handle a specific issue in my relationship?

A: There isn't one. Win by Losing is a lifestyle choice. That means it's a way of communicating in your relationship. It's not a specific intervention to fix a particular issue. Adopting the Win by Losing method, and communicating in a way which is consistent with the five Relationship Enablers, will enable you to tackle the issue at hand.

Multiple Choice

1. Taking time to stop and think about what I want from my relationship is important because:

    a. I am much more likely to get what I want from my relationship when it's clear to me what those things are.

    b. Thinking about it will make it happen.

    c.   I can write it down and hand the list to my partner who will do everything she can to make those things a reality for me.

    d.   I can spend time chatting with my friends about these things even though they can't actually do anything about them.

2. Win By Losing applies to me when:

    a.   I am in a steady relationship.

    b.   I have just met someone and want to communicate with them in an effective way.

    c.   I have just split up with someone and am enjoying the freedom that brings.

    d.   All of the above.

3. Win By Losing applies to the following contexts:

    a.   Developing my career.

    b.   Dealing with persistent sales calls.

    c.   Communicating with my intimate partner.

    d.   Resolving a problem between me and a family member.

4. When we mention intimacy in this book, what do we mean?

    a.   Holding hands.

    b.   Having a shower together.

    c.   Making up after an argument.

    d.   Whatever is right for me and my partner.

5. The way in which men communicate with the modern Western woman has changed relatively recently because:

    a.   A battle between the sexes has been raging since the 1960s and women have won.

    b.   Relatively recent changes in technology and society have created an environment in which women enjoy greater freedom, independence, and choice than ever before. With this in mind, the best way for men to have happy intimate relationships with women is to adopt the Win by Losing method.

   c. Government legislation has given women more power in the bedroom.

   d. Nothing else has really happened in the past 100 years.

Take Action

Take some time to answer and act upon the following questions.

1. What do you want from your relationship? What makes you happy?

   - Write down a list of 3–5 things that you want from your relationship. Keep it simple because overcomplicating it sets you up for failure.

   - Put your list away and look at it in a few days' time. Are you sure these things will make you happy in your relationship? It's worth giving this some thought and ensuring the list is right for you.

   - How many of your points are being met fully right now? If some, or all, aren't being met, read on!

2. What is the difference between active and passive reading? What will you do to ensure you read actively?

   - Answer each of the questions in the Q&A section before checking your understanding is correct?

   - Complete the Multiple Choice section (answers are available in Appendix 2)?

   - Write down your responses to the 'Take Action' section at the end of every chapter?

   - Carry out all or some of our exercises?

- Utilize the 90-day action plan available in Appendix 1?

- A combination of these things?

3. There is no best time to read this book. What are your circumstances right now?

   - If you are in a difficult relationship which you would like to improve, what makes the relationship difficult? How could the way you communicate together change in order for you to be happy?

   - If you are in a happy relationship which you feel could be even better, what needs to change?

   - If you are single, what are you looking for in your next relationship? And how open are you to handling your communication differently next time?

4. What does "intimacy" mean to you?

   - This term is open to interpretation, but what does it mean to you right now?

   - Is your relationship at the level of intimacy which works best for you? If not, you need to read the rest of this book before addressing this issue.

5. Why is Win by Losing a lifestyle choice?

   - If you have read this chapter, you will know the answer!

   - Are you open to the idea of adopting a new approach to communicating with your partner? If yes, keep reading in an active way.

What's Next?

In the next chapter we will define in detail the Win by Losing Method.

CHAPTER 2

What is Win by Losing?

A relationship is like a house. When a light bulb burns out you do not go and buy a new house, you change the light bulb.

ANONYMOUS

Why read this chapter? What's in it for you?

In this chapter we will cover:

- ▶ What's most important: The "Win" in Win by Losing;
- ▶ A limited supply: Your Emotional Energy;
- ▶ Don't throw it all away: Understanding why relationships end;
- ▶ Power in your hands: Take control and don't be treated like a doormat;
- ▶ Key Points;
- ▶ Questions and Answers;
- ▶ Multiple Choice;
- ▶ Take Action;
- ▶ What's Next?

Let's make a start: Introduction

Win by Losing is a method which, when utilized correctly, in the right context and alongside the Relationship Enablers (see Chapters 3 – 8), will enable you to enjoy much happier and more meaningful relationships. This is achieved by communicating with your partner in a more effective manner.

Where intimate relationships are concerned, better communication always leads to better results.

What do we mean by the *Win by Losing method*? This is a set of tools and techniques that will help you to handle a multitude of situations effectively. This will enable you to eliminate conflict, understand your partner's thinking, and achieve what you **want and need** from your relationship. This method is a way of communicating which will allow you to deal productively with the situation at hand.

We are only concerned with our thoughts, the words we choose to say and the way we say those words. When an effective communication method is in place, the associated positive behaviors will naturally follow. Without an effective method, we won't know what constructive words to say when communicating with our partner and will become distracted, irritated and annoyed.

Where intimate relationships are concerned, we depend on having an effective method to deal with the situation at hand.

To understand the Win by Losing method, we must first cover these four topics:

1. Emotional Energy

2. Sink of Negativity

3. Ground Rules

4. Balance of Power

Topic 1 – A Limited Supply: Your Emotional Energy

We all have different types of energy, levels of fitness and strength. Some of us work out in the gym and eat in a healthy way, which normally leads to being fit and healthy. But another type of energy is what we call "Emotional Energy;" that is, the type of energy we use when tackling any type of emotional issue in our lives. We use this type of energy, when disagreeing and arguing with our partner, among other things.

What's important is that each of us has what can best be described as a rechargeable battery which contains our Emotional Energy, and loses charge over time. Although there are individual differences where some of us have a high-capacity 9-volt battery and others a much smaller AAA-size battery (determined mainly by our childhood experiences), women have higher-capacity batteries than men, and crucially are also able to recharge their Emotional Energy batteries far more quickly than men too.

Most women have super-powerful fast-recharge Emotional Energy batteries compared to the average man.

This means that when a man and his partner have an argument and the disagreement continues over a period of time, once his Emotional Energy battery is exhausted, the man is ready to move on. However, the woman, with far more energy available in her higher-capacity, fast-recharge battery, can remain focused and motivated for considerably longer, in order to achieve her preferred outcome. More often than not, the man will eventually just agree with his partner, mainly because he really doesn't care anymore. Typically, the woman will get her way eventually.

This is just a fact of life and has nothing to do with men normally being physically stronger than women. Note also that women aren't actually doing anything wrong here—they are simply utilizing their larger and faster-recharging Emotional Energy batteries in exactly the same way men would, if they had the opportunity.

A tough reality to accept: Why women have the Emotional Energy advantage

The unfortunate truth that men need to understand is that because women are able to recharge their larger and longer lasting Emotional Energy batteries more quickly than men, it means women are the stronger gender from an Emotional Energy perspective. Remember we are only concerned with the context of intimate relationships, so don't start generalizing and applying these explanations to different contexts such as politics or work.

The typical woman's Emotional Energy batteries will recharge more quickly and last for longer than the typical man's.

That's why the various examples given in the Prelude may have been familiar to you. Men who don't understand that they are doomed to lose certain arguments are battling in vain. They may win the argument but will inevitably lose in the longer term. The typical man will give in eventually, even when he doesn't even know he's doing it.

With reference to the second scenario cited in the Prelude, when Jane eventually got the soft furnishings she wanted, Peter probably went with her to purchase them. At the time it wouldn't have felt like *losing*, because the context of the argument had disappeared. By then, Peter might have even convinced himself that he also wanted the throw and brightly colored cushions. But he had well and truly lost. He didn't need to lose though; he could have recognized the situation at the outset and won at that point, by realizing where the argument was heading and agreeing with Jane's preference. Then he could have Won by Losing. Any other option was doomed to failure.

Why is this the case? Why do women, generally speaking, have higher-capacity and faster-recharging Emotional Energy batteries than men? Let's consider very briefly how men and women evolved. Without wanting to oversimplify the matter, in ancient times, men made the tools needed to hunt and went out hunting to bring back food for the family to survive. Men protected women from other men and predators, to ensure the home was safe and secure. They taught their sons the skills needed to survive in the context of a violent and physical world. These male activities were essential, as they enabled women to focus on cooking, cleaning, bringing up children and looking after the home.

These were the traditional responsibilities of the woman which, of course, are rightly becoming less applicable in modern, liberal democracies.

In ancient times women needed a truly astonishing level of Emotional Energy to bring up children in a primitive world. If you have children in this modern age, you will know how hard it is, but imagine having to manage with no running hot or cold water, no electricity, no toilet, central heating and certainly no air-conditioning. It redefines the term "tough." If that doesn't give you an insight into just how tough women had to be in order to survive, nothing will.

The fact that society has developed, along with the technology upon which we all depend, has done nothing to reduce the Emotional Energy of the typical woman. It's in their genes. The women who did not have this type of endurance to bring up their children in ancient times died out a long time ago.

Women didn't raise children on their own. They needed help, which came from other women. Together they ran their homes, cooked food, and brought up their children. Fast-forward to today. Who in the relationship normally coordinates the social calendar? Sure, men have a say, but we think you will find it's the woman who makes most of the social arrangements.

Modern technology has removed the need for physical strength to survive. Nobody in the Western world has to hunt for their dinner, and most Western women certainly don't need to rely on men to survive.

It's no coincidence that when a marriage ends, more often than not it's the woman who retains the social bonds rather than the man. The man is more likely to lose the family home, most of his friends, and sometimes even his mind when the security of his life (created mainly by his partner) crumbles around him.

What does this mean? It means women are far better at discussing their emotions with other women and, more importantly for our discussion, it means they are able to recharge their high-capacity Emotional Energy batteries more quickly than men. They are primed and ready for the next round of arguments and to focus better on getting what they want. They won't give up and will keep pushing, no matter how much Emotional Energy is needed, or how long it will take. From a man's perspective they are relentless—they just won't "let it go."

Topic 2 – Why relationships end: Sink of Negativity

It's time to fill your kitchen sink (see Figure 2.1). Put in the plug and watch the water level rise as the water pours out of the faucets (taps). Your sink is a representation of a relationship. When you first meet, the sink is empty. Then one day, something happens and you have your first argument.

Each time you have an argument you run some water into the sink. One of you starts an argument and the faucets open. The type of argument and what is said during that argument determine how much water is released into the sink. Eventually the argument comes to an end and the faucets close. Sometimes the argument lingers and continues as bickering, so drops of water keep dripping out of the faucet. Other times the argument truly comes to an end and water stops entering the sink.

As time goes by, you have positive experiences with your partner: You go out to dinner, go shopping, have days out together and meet up with friends and family. Each of these experiences opens the sink plug and removes some of the water from the sink. Time goes on and water is added and water is taken away. The faucets open and close; the plug opens and closes. The water level rises and falls.

One day, there is an argument about something which seems relatively unimportant, such as what to have for dinner or what movie to see at the movie theater. Somehow this blows up into a larger argument about pretty much everything important to you both in your relationship, and the next thing is that one of you announces that you have had enough and the relationship is over. The sink is full and the water has finally overflowed.

When the water overflows due to the sink being full, the relationship always ends. It might not end there and then, as our lives can become complex and entangled, but it's only a matter of time before a parting of ways.

To complicate matters, beyond a certain water-level height, it is no longer possible to let out any more water. The plug jams shut. If you have ever experienced the final months of an unhappy relationship, you will understand what we mean. Each argument just adds more water. The relationship is going downhill and only inertia maintains it until its inevitable conclusion.

Even changes to the way you communicate and agreements between the two of you which, in normal times would unplug the sink, fail to move the plug as it is simply too late. Each argument makes matters worse and there is nothing you can do to reduce the friction between you.

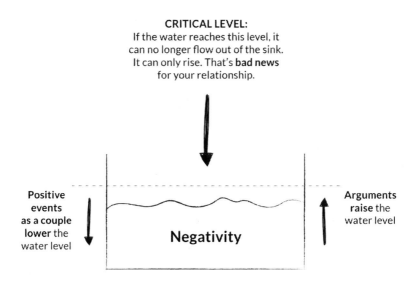

Figure 2.1. Sink of Negativity

The water level isn't only determined by the good times and the bad—it's determined by everything which happens between you. Absolutely everything: Every comment, every time you interact together, every discussion, every agreement, every text you send each other, every time you touch each other, every disagreement, every time you work as a team or against each other.

Every interaction can be classified as positive, neutral, or negative. Positive interactions lower the water level; neutral interactions have no effect and negative interactions raise the water level. You can communicate with each other from different parts of the planet and still these communications, unless they are neutral, will raise or lower the water level in the Sink of Negativity.

We can also express the way in which negativity impacts on relationships in terms of an *emotional* joint bank account. Each time you have a positive interaction together you make a joint *deposit* into the account. On the other hand, every time there is friction or an argument, there's an emotional *withdrawal*. Things can become pretty bumpy in relationships and you will be pleased to hear that an overdraft facility is available. However, if you go overdrawn over and above your overdraft limit, then you both go bankrupt with the associated ending of your relationship.

> *When matters between you become intolerable for both of you, when there is that much bad feeling, there is no way back.*

It is ridiculously easy to convey a *negative* message to your partner. Negativity has a seemingly self-perpetuating energy and remains in our minds, influencing our thoughts and therefore the way we communicate, long after an argument has ended. We play out what we *could* have said, *should* have said, and *will* say in the future when the opportunity presents itself.

Contrast this to *positive* messages which close the faucets, open the plug, and allow the water level to lower. It's just as easy to give a compliment, tell your partner that you love her, or demonstrate your love by supporting her in the mundane tasks of life.

Honestly speaking, which do you focus on? There can be a tendency to focus more on the negative, but this will eventually lead to a full sink and the end of the relationship. If this is not the direction you want, you need to make an active and conscious decision to change your focus. Change to the positive. Win by Losing. The choice is yours.

Topic 3 – What's most important to you: Ground Rules

Although we go into considerably more detail on "ground rules" in Chapter 4, in brief your ground rules are those things which are most important to you in your relationship and in your life. Rather than a long and unobtainable wish list, it's a short list of those things which really matter to you.

For some men that might mean that one night of the week is reserved for drinks with their buddies, or having a space at home which they can call their own—their "man cave"—and for others, it could mean having time to work out regularly at the gym, play a musical instrument, or perhaps pursue an interest in photography.

Ground rules can also include statements which govern the way you interact with your partner, such as, "There are always things to do. Just write them in a list and leave them to me. I don't need reminding and will get them done over the next few weeks."

Most people have a built-in understanding and appreciation of fairness. Ground rules must be fair and reasonable – they should never be used as an excuse to control your partner.

*Ground rules must **never** force your partner to do something she doesn't want to do. It's unfair, unreasonable and will fill your partner's Sink of Negativity.*

Your ground rules will be unique to you. Whatever your ground rules are, the list should be kept short with no more than four or five items. Any more than this and you won't have the Emotional Energy needed to enforce them.

As far as Win by Losing is concerned, ensuring your partner adheres to your ground rules is fundamental to the success of your relationship. These are your ground rules and are not open to discussion, compromise, or negotiation.

Topic 4 – Balance of power: Nobody's in control

In a healthy and happy relationship there is a sustainable balance of power between you. However, an imbalance will create unnecessary tension and will ultimately fill the Sink of Negativity.

Power imbalance = rising tension = more water in the Sink of Negativity.

How does this imbalance of power show itself in a relationship? This can be explained in one word: "Control."

A man has never turned to his partner and said, "I love the way you control what I do and when I do it. Stopping me from doing what's important to me, just because you can, leaves me feeling so good about myself and our relationship."

Equally, a woman has never turned to her partner and said, "Your ability to control me is truly wonderful. You should do it more."

Neither of you should be in a position of control. It may feel good for the one in control in the short term, but will ultimately lead to an unhappy relationship for both of you. Where one party has more control in a relationship than the other, this will inevitably lead to friction between you which will raise the water level in the Sink of Negativity.

Happy relationships are about partnership.

How do you ensure a sustainable balance of power between you? Respect for each other's ground rules. Neither party can control the other if they have respect for the other's ground rules and allow these to be enforced properly. How can one person control the other and respect their ground rules at the same time? It's not possible.

Respect for each other's ground rules supports a fair balance of power in your relationship which, in turn, will ensure long-term healthy communication between you, and a happy relationship together.

There is no *rule* for how much power one party should have compared to the other. It's what is right and works for the two of you. One couple's balance of power is not necessarily the same as another's. It's simple really: If the balance of power between you and your partner makes you both happy, neither party has too much control over the other and you both respect each other's ground rules, then all is well as far as the balance of power in your relationship is concerned.

Bringing the 4 topics together: The "Win" in Win by Losing

So, what's the "Win" in Win by Losing? That depends on what's most important to you in your relationship and in your life right now. Whatever your ground rules, having the things in your life which bring you happiness is your version of winning.

If, for example, your ground rules include having time to meet your buddies for drinks every week, or time to learn a musical instrument, then having those things in your life, no matter what else is happening where your relationship is concerned, is your version of winning. It doesn't matter what your partner would prefer you to do; these are your ground rules and are not open to discussion, compromise, or negotiation.

Ensuring you are able to do whatever is important to you is your version of winning. Your ground rules are not open to discussion, compromise, or negotiation.

Preserving your Emotional Energy: How you 'win' in Win by Losing

You "win" in Win by Losing by choosing your battles wisely and not wasting your Emotional Energy on matters which are unrelated to your ground rules.

Ensuring your partner adheres to your ground rules is fundamental to the success of your relationship, as this also ensures a happy and sustainable balance of power between the two of you.

By enforcing your ground rules, you also ensure you don't turn into a doormat, for when this happens, the balance of power between you becomes unsustainable and your relationship will eventually end anyway.

Where everything else is concerned, including all matters unrelated to your ground rules, adopt the Win by Losing method and ensure you communicate in a way which is consistent with the Relationship Enablers (see Chapters 3 – 8).

You can win in your relationship by identifying those conversations which are likely to morph into an argument about something unrelated to your ground rules. They are a waste of Emotional Energy and you will probably eventually lose.

As we have established, women use their Emotional Energy to regularly get their way because they don't give up and they continue until they achieve the outcome they wanted, long after the typical man has lost interest and moved on. The more heated the argument, the more you turn the issue into a win–lose scenario, and the greater the fall when you lose the argument, either in the short or, more likely, long term.

A better approach is to win by foreseeing what's about to happen and use our method for a better outcome. Unless it's absolutely necessary and related directly to enforcing one of your ground rules, don't let the conversation turn into an unnecessary argument as this wastes your Emotional Energy which you should save for when it's really needed.

If you are not willing to invest all your Emotional Energy into winning the argument, you have to ask yourself what's in it for you. The whole point of having an argument is to win, not run out of Emotional Energy before your partner does, and then find that you have lost.

Choose your arguments wisely and concentrate all your Emotional Energy into winning arguments concerned with enforcing your ground rules. That's the "win" in Win by Losing. Don't let a conversation become an argument unless you need to enforce a ground rule, nothing is gained and your Emotional Energy is wasted.

The Win by Losing Method

Figure 2.2 presents the Win by Losing Method, and depicts the Win by Losing approach to communication. The image shows the five Relationship Enabler pillars which rest upon the Win by Losing Method. A Happy Relationship—meaning one which provides happiness to both parties— rests on the five pillars.

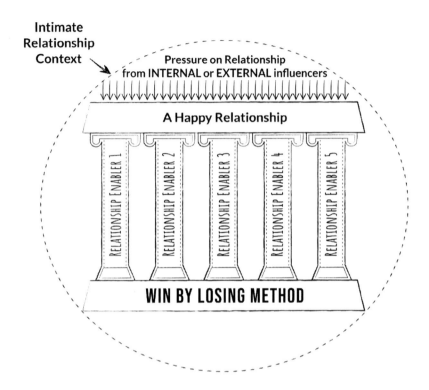

Figure 2.2. The Win by Losing Method: Supporting your relationship properly

Internal pressure from your and your partner's values, beliefs, and expectations of the relationship, along with external pressures such as family, friends, money, and kids, press down on the model, putting pressure on the Relationship Enablers and the Win by Losing method. The model resides within the context of intimate relationships, shown as a circle. Keep in mind that this model will not work in other contexts such as work, with friends or family, as the dynamics in those relationships are completely different.

Clearly, relationships are more likely to become damaged and end during those challenging times when the pressure builds.

The stereotypical holiday romance has no pressure applied to it until life returns to normal. In most, but not all cases, it can quickly crumble under normal conditions. Having solid foundations to the way you communicate together is key to forming mutually happy relationships. The importance of strong foundations is clear and we will discuss the Relationship Enablers in Chapters 3 – 8, as they are an integral part of the Win by Losing method.

It's not just about you: Three Emotional Sinks

Figure 2.3 reveals three emotional sinks rather than one. The sink in the top-left corner represents *your* personal sink, where your relationship is concerned. The sink next to it on the right represents *your partner's* sink. Water from both sinks flow into the sink at the bottom which is *the relationship's* sink. With this approach, if any one of the sinks overflow the relationship ends.

Throughout the remainder of this book we will refer to the Sink of Negativity. Depending on the context of the topic under consideration this could be your sink, your partner's sink, or the relationship's joint sink. Rather than go into detail each time (which can become repetitive) we will just refer to the Sink of Negativity.

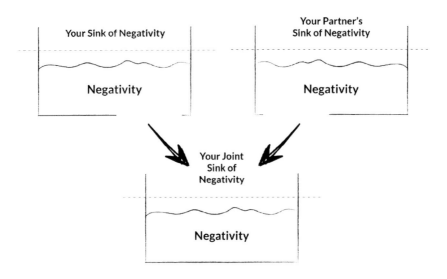

Figure 2.3. Three Emotional Sinks

What happens if your sink or your partner's sink is almost ready to overflow? This could occur when some people have affairs. Not ending the relationship may seem easier than ending it, as it avoids any messiness with heartache, kids, and money. It's not unusual to hear about someone in a relationship having an affair and the other party not knowing about it for years. This is probably where one party's sink is almost ready to overflow, but their partner's sink is not.

You can't read your partner's mind—ask them how the relationship is going from their point of view. It's a great way to find out!

Putting it all together: Win by Losing

By combining the Sink of Negativity and the Win by Losing method, and introducing the idea of four drains allowing water out of our sink (see Figure 2.4), we are able show you how it all fits together. You may have been asking yourself how the negative energy drains out of the sink. There are four different drains and we will discuss each one briefly.

As you can see in Figure 2.4, the higher the water level, the more pressure is applied to the structure upon which your happiness rests.

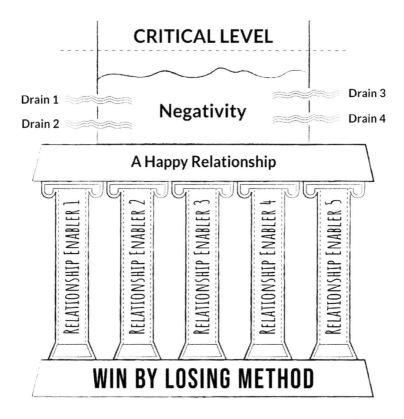

Figure 2.4. Putting it all together: Win by Losing

As with every structure there is a limit to the amount of pressure the columns can take before they start to crumble and, ultimately, fail.

As shown in Figure 2.4, four drains have been added to the sink, and represent the following:

- *Drain 1*: *Have a plan and take action.* As mentioned in Chapter 1: Introduction, for the content of this book to make a genuine difference, you need to take action. We appreciate this is not as straightforward as it sounds. The *Take Action* sections at the end of every chapter, along with Chapter 10: Don't just sit there: How to put Win by Losing into Practice and Appendix 1: Your 90-Day Action Plan will help you to put this material into practice, so that it makes a positive difference to the way you communicate with your partner, and therefore, to the way you relate to each other. Taking action will open our first drain and release negative energy.

- *Drain 2*: *Mutual understanding, respect, and enforcing each other's ground rules.* Having a high level of mutual respect for ground rules, as described in Chapter 2: What is Win by Losing? will ensure this drain will flow easily. It means those aspects in your relationship and in your life that are most important to you continue uninterrupted, despite the challenges life has in store for both of you.

- *Drain 3*: *Talk it through.* When difficulties fill your sink, talk them through. Don't let them fester as issues are only resolved through dialogue. Like the other drains, this can easily become blocked. All the Relationship Enablers (Chapters 3 – 8) play their part in helping you to talk things through in a calm, focused, and constructive manner.

- *Drain 4*: *Residue from old unresolved issues.* Talking through any old issues which may exist between you and your partner will open this drain and lower the water level. The following chapters will greatly assist you in this respect:

  - Chapter 5 – Make every conversation matter: Listening with Intent;

  - Chapter 7 – Just Accept It: Acceptance of what we can and cannot change;

- Chapter 8 – Say what you mean: Straight Talking.

A healthy balance of power: You are not a doormat!

It's important to distinguish between the Win by Losing method and being treated like a doormat. The two are completely different and not to be confused.

Win by Losing is about learning to identify most of the disagreements and arguments which happen during the normal course of your relationship, accepting your partner will get her way in most cases eventually, and avoiding those arguments in the first place. This method ensures you don't waste your Emotional Energy and instead preserve it to enforce your ground rules.

It's not about becoming a doormat and allowing your partner to take total control of your relationship. There must always be a fair and healthy balance of power and mutual respect between you.

Identify those unimportant things which don't matter and make a choice not to waste your Emotional Energy arguing about them. #dontfightalosingbattle.

Don't turn a molehill into a mountain: Zero-sum game

The Win by Losing method can be explained in terms of the *Zero-Sum Game*, where your gain or loss is balanced exactly by your partner's gain or loss. This means you have as much to lose as your partner has to gain.

The more you have to lose, the more she has to gain; the greater the stakes, the further you could fall.

Men who play to win all of the time set themselves up for a fall from a great height by wasting their Emotional Energy. The Win by Losing method ensures there is no fall. Of course, where enforcing your ground rules is concerned, when you invest all your Emotional Energy, there is the small risk of a considerable fall, but you have minimized that risk by ensuring you have the Emotional Energy needed to win when it really matters.

Lose by Losing: The 80:20 rule

There are times where the Win by Losing method really is losing and that can only damage your relationship. This can be explained in terms of the *80:20 Rule*, where the most common event will take place to 80 percent of people, 80 percent of the time.

This book applies to 80 percent of people, 80 percent of the time.

Here, we are concerned with the 20 percent of exceptions. If you find that you have to become a doormat for peace with your partner at any cost, then you need to give some serious thought about the type of relationship you are in and how this could be changed.

From a Win by Losing perspective there are only two options:

1. Enforce your ground rules consistently, which you have communicated clearly to your partner. Without clearly communicated and mutually respected ground rules, the power imbalance between you will become too great to sustain the relationship in the longer term. This means the relationship will eventually come to an end, but not before months or even years of unnecessary unhappiness.

2. Leave your partner.

As the Irish playwright, George Bernard Shaw, said:

It is a curious sensation: the sort of pain that goes mercifully beyond our powers of feeling. When your heart is broken, your boats are burned: nothing matters any more. It is the end of happiness and the beginning of peace.

But what does that mean? In the final days or months of a relationship in terminal decline, we know what's happening to us. Quite often, when the relationship eventually comes to an end, despite other ramifications it may have on our life at that time, it's not uncommon to experience a sense of relief.

The anticipation is over and the arguments too.

No matter where you are in your relationship, whether or not you are married, whether or not you have children, any ending of a relationship signifies change. All change is difficult and there may be many hurdles to overcome. In spite of this, the end of a relationship always opens up new possibilities and opportunities. In most, but not all cases, the difference between the person who doesn't *move on* compared to the person who carves out a new life for themselves is more to do with their focus and determination rather than anything else.

We all have the ability to *move on* when a relationship comes to an end. It's a decision which might not happen straightaway, but the time will come when we decide to explore new avenues in our lives. Women tend to make the choice to move on more quickly than men and are more decisive when their choice is made. This isn't because they are any less caring than men, but is a combination of their Emotional Energy and better developed social network, which support them through these challenging times.

You've Reached This Far: The end of Chapter two

By this stage, you should now understand what we mean by Win by Losing, ground rules, the importance of preserving your Emotional Energy, and why the Sink of Negativity is so important to intimate relationships.

Don't stop now! Spend a little time reading the Key Points for this chapter along with the Q&As, Multiple Choice questions, and 'Take Action' questions for you to consider and act upon.

Chapter 3 introduces what we mean by Relationship Enablers, with each having a subsequent chapter to itself. There's so much more to cover.

Key Points

1. The Win by Losing method is an approach for handling communication in a positive way with your partner. It's all about saving your Emotional Energy to enforce your ground rules in an effective way and will lead to better outcomes for both of you. Remember your ground rules are not open to discussion, compromise, or negotiation.

2. Physical strength is completely different from emotional strength. Most women have larger and faster-charging Emotional Energy batteries than the average man. Win by Losing addresses this issue in a positive way.

3. You "Win" by adopting the Win by Losing method and communicating in a way which is consistent with the five Relationship Enablers.

4. A healthy balance of power through respect for each other's ground rules is a prerequisite for a happy and long-lasting relationship. Neither of you should have control over the other.

5. The Sink of Negativity will fill when you and your partner communicate in a negative way, and will empty when you communicate in a positive way. When the water reaches a certain level, it can no longer flow out of the sink. When the water level overflows, the relationship ends.

6. Don't be a doormat. Win by Losing is about getting what you want out of your relationship. If your partner doesn't respect you, ask yourself why you are with her in the first place.

7. A happy relationship relies upon communicating in a manner which is consistent with the Relationship Enablers and the Win by Losing method.

8. Referring to the prelude, it doesn't matter if you are a Fred, Peter, Jim, Ryan, or a combination of these characters. It doesn't matter if you are completely different from all four of them. The Win by Losing method will work for you. Win by Losing. The choice is yours.

Questions and Answers

Q: What is Emotional Energy?

A: It's the type of energy we need to deal with emotional issues in our lives. We use this energy, among other things, when arguing with our partners. Women have larger-capacity and faster recharging Emotional Energy batteries than men, which means that you need to save this type of energy for when you really need it.

Q: What is the "Win" in Win by Losing?

A: Preserving your Emotional Energy so you are able to enforce your ground rules and get what you want from your relationship is your version of winning.

Q: Is Win by Losing all about avoiding arguments and doing what I'm told?

A: No. It is not about turning you into a doormat. It's about saving your Emotional Energy for the arguments you need to have, in order to enforce your ground rules. Get that right and everything else will fall into place.

Q: So Win by Losing is about choosing my arguments wisely. Is that it?

A: Not entirely. It's also about communicating in a way which is consistent with the five Relationship Enablers (see Chapters 3 – 8).

Q: Why do you focus on communication rather than behavior?

A: The behavior we experience in our relationships is a consequence of the way we communicate. Get the communication right and the behavior between the two of you will follow.

Q: What is the Zero-Sum Game?

A: In Win By Losing it means the more you have to lose in an argument, the more your partner has to win. You can make either your or your partner's win bigger by raising the stakes and having a bigger argument—the bigger the argument, the greater the stakes; the greater the stakes, the bigger the potential fall.

Q: What is the Sink of Negativity?

A: It's a way of explaining what happens to intimate relationships when negative events outweigh positive ones.

Q: Does being right mean I will win the argument?

A: No. Winning an argument with your partner is all about who has the Emotional Energy to win. Arguments normally end because one or both parties don't have the type of energy needed to carry on, not because one party agreed the other was right.

Q: Men are physically stronger than women. Surely this means they are emotionally stronger too?

A: Physical strength has nothing to do with emotional strength. For a variety of historical and biological reasons, women have the edge over men where emotional strength is concerned. Win by Losing addresses this issue in a positive way for both men and women.

Q: Is there one emotional sink in the relationship or three?

A: There are three: Yours, your partner's, and the relationship's. The negativity from your and your partner's sinks flow into the relationship's sink.

Q: What are the drains in the emotional sink, and why do they matter?

A: The drains allow negative energy to flow away from the emotional sink. They matter because, if the negative energy overflows, the relationship will end. The drains are:

1. Having a plan and take action;

2. Mutual understanding, respect, and enforcing each other's ground rules;

3. Talk it through;

4. Residue from old unresolved issues.

Multiple Choice

1. Win by Losing is a way to:

    a. Force your partner to do what you want.

    b. Communicate with your partner in a more constructive way.

    c. Ensure you are treated like a doormat, so you do everything you are told.

    d. Approach your next salary review.

2. Your Emotional Energy is important because:

    a. Women's rechargeable batteries, which hold this type of energy, have a larger capacity and recharge more quickly than the average man's.

    b. You can use it in the gym to become fit and healthy in half the usual time.

    c. You can sell it on eBay for a healthy profit.

    d. It's a measure of your personal strength and fitness.

3.   In the context of this book, the Win by Losing method is:

   a.   A way of winning chess.

   b.   A new approach to getting on better with your partner's friends and parents.

   c.   An effective way of communicating with your partner, leading to happier times together.

   d.   The answer to your employer's dreams. A new approach which will guarantee you achieve their overly ambitious targets this year.

4.   You go shopping with your partner for a new sofa and she has decided on the color. Do you:

   a.   Insist on your preferred color as you can't stand the thought of the settee being anything else?

   b.   Phone your mother so she can make the final decision?

   c.   Accept that, as there are more important things in your relationship to deal with (unless the color of your sofa is one of your ground rules), you will agree with her preferred choice?

   d.   Phone your partner's mother so she can make the final decision?

5.   When the Sink of Negativity overflows, what happens to your relationship?

   a.   It brings you closer together.

   b.   It causes the relationship to end.

   c.   It reduces the amount of arguments you have together.

   d.   Nothing.

6.   The drains in the Sink of Negativity:

   a.   Help to fill the sink with more negativity.

   b.   Keep the sink clean and tidy.

c. Are normally blocked and can only be cleared with a good argument.

d. Enable the negative energy to flow away, thereby lowering the water level and pressure on the relationship.

7. Women normally have a greater level of Emotional Energy than men because:

a. Important historical and psychological factors developed their cognitive abilities in this way.

b. They attend secret Emotional Energy gyms.

c. They were lucky.

d. None of this is true and it's actually all about physical strength.

Take Action

Please take some time to answer and act upon these questions.

1. Write down three examples where you lost an argument with your partner because you simply ran out of Emotional Energy.

    • All men have plenty of examples so don't kid yourself that you have none!

    • Given what we have covered in this chapter, how could you have handled those situations differently? Would the long-term outcome have been any different?

2. How might you choose your battles more wisely in the future?

    • What does that mean about those arguments which, when you stop to think about it, were about things that weren't important to you?

    • How will this approach impact your relationship right now?

3. What are your ground rules?

- Make a list of those things which matter the most to you in your relationship and life. These are the things worth arguing about!

- Have you ever argued about issues which are *not* on your list? Why? How did the argument work out? Was it worth it?

4. Are you treated like a doormat?

- If yes, why do you think that is the case? Is there mutual respect in your relationship?

- What simple ground rules could you put in place to stop this from happening in the future?

- How will you communicate your ground rules to your partner? Read about the Relationship Enablers (Chapters 3–8) before having this type of conversation.

5. If you have had an unhappy breakup in the past, why did your Sink of Negativity overflow?

- Provide three examples where negativity was added to the sink.

- Given what you know about the Win by Losing method, how could this have been handled differently?

6. Positive communication and experiences together reduce the water level in your Sink of Negativity.

- Make a list of between three and six actions you can take over the next week to reduce the water level in your relationship's Sink of Negativity.

- Review the list in a week's time. Did you complete all your actions? If so, in what way has this affected the way the two of you communicate? If not, why not? And what will you do differently in future?

7. Given what you now know about Emotional Energy, how might you handle friction or an argument in the future?

    -   Thinking about the disagreements and arguments you have with your partner; which are worth having? What about the others?

    -   Which disagreements and arguments are better handled by adopting the Win by Losing method?

    -   How would adopting the Win by Losing method change the ultimate outcome of your arguments?

    -   List the advantages and disadvantages to you of adopting the Win by Losing method.

8. Over the next week or two, write down each time you saved your Emotional Energy and when you needed to use it.

    -   Describe how you were better able to win when you had pre-served your Emotional Energy for when it was really needed.

    -   If you were unable to preserve your Emotional Energy, were you really adopting the Win by Losing method, and only arguing to enforce your ground rules? See Chapter 4 for more information and detail on ground rules.

    -   How has adopting the Win by Losing method changed the way you communicate with your partner? How has it changed the way your partner communicates with you? What has been the effect on your Sink of Negativity?

    -   All change takes time and, if it's a new approach, adopting the Win by Losing method will also take time to become second nature to you. It will also take time for your partner to adjust to your new way of communicating. What have you learned about applying the Win by Losing method to the way you communicate every day? What changes, if any, have you experienced as a result of adopting this approach?

What further changes would you like to achieve? How do you plan to achieve these further changes?

What's Next?

In the next chapter we will introduce you to the concept of Relationship Enablers which are a vital part of the Win by Losing Method.

PART II
Relationship Enablers

CHAPTER 3

Relationship Enablers: An Introduction

When I saw you, I fell in love, and you smiled because you knew.

ARRIGO BOITO, ITALIAN POET

Why read this chapter? What's in it for you?

In this chapter we will cover:

- ► An explanation: What are Relationship Enablers?
- ► Arguments don't resolve underlying issues: Relationship Enablers in action;
- ► Let's start again: Why Relationships are so much easier at the outset;
- ► A happy outcome: Why not Win-Win in your relationship?
- ► Key Points;
- ► Questions and Answers;
- ► Multiple Choice;
- ► Take Action;
- ► What's Next?

An explanation: What are Relationship Enablers?

Relationship Enablers are positive ways of communicating with your partner. As outlined in Chapter 1, they are:

1. **I won't back down: Enforce your Ground Rules** (Chapter 4): Ground Rules are the most important things to you in your life and relationship. Enforcing them ensures they stay in place.

2. **Make every conversation matter: Listening with Intent** (Chapter 5): A way of listening to your partner which encourages effective communication.

3. **We're in this together: Common Purpose** (Chapter 6): Understanding why you are in a relationship together to ensure you both achieve the outcomes you desire.

4. **Just accept it: Acceptance of what we can and cannot change** (Chapter 7): No matter how much you love your partner, you can't change her. Change can only come from within you.

5. **Say what you mean: Straight Talking** (Chapter 8): Saying what's really on your mind in a calm and constructive manner.

Adopting the Win by Losing method and communicating in a way which is consistent with the five Relationship Enablers ensures a far happier relationship as the water level in your three Sinks of Negativity (yours; your partner's; the relationship's) will decline over time. See Chapter 2 for an explanation of the Sinks of Negativity. Relationship Enablers are the fundamental supporting structures on which all relationships are based, and determine whether both you and your partner experience happiness as a consequence of being together.

Relationship Enablers and the culture of an organization have something in common: They both exist whether or not we are aware of their existence, or understand what they are. Large organizations spend considerable sums of money on discovering their culture so that they can improve it in some way. The fact that there may have been a time where the culture was not clearly defined doesn't detract from there having been a culture in place, which has an impact on much of what happens among staff, departments, and customers.

"Culture eats strategy for breakfast," is a phrase originated by Peter Drucker, an American management consultant, and made famous by Mark Fields, President at Ford Motors. It means that no matter how clever or important the plans are for the future development of an organization, if the culture does not support the change, then any attempt to implement change will ultimately fail. Perhaps that's why there are so many examples of failed change programs littering the commercial world.

The same can be said of relationships; if the importance of communicating in a way which is consistent with the Relationship Enablers is not appreciated, simply adopting the Win by Losing method will not be enough to lead to the desired outcome of being in a happy relationship.

Adopt the Win by Losing method and communicate in a way which is consistent with the five Relationship Enablers, in order to transform your relationship.

The way we communicate and the habits we develop all take place early on in a relationship, when times are easy and these things don't matter to us, and are consistent with some of the Relationship Enablers to a greater or lesser extent, but not with others. When times become challenging, often we only react to the symptom rather than the cause. The most common symptom is friction between you, which manifests through bickering and arguments.

None of these symptoms solve the underlying issues caused by a failure to communicate in a way which is consistent with all five Relationship Enablers. Nobody has ever turned around to their partner and said, "We should argue more regularly... it brings us closer and really helps to clear the air."

Unfortunately, the closer our emotional bonds are to our partner, the more difficult it becomes to separate the symptoms from the underlying cause.

Those relationship pressures we all feel: Internal and external influencers

Relationships don't exist in a vacuum. If they did, everything would be so much simpler and it wouldn't matter whether or not your communication was consistent with the five Relationship Enablers. This, however, is not the case. *External* influences such as family, marriage, kids, money, and career all play their part. *Internal* influencers consist of the pressure we all put on our relationships, due to our own values, beliefs, and expectations, both of our relationship and ourselves. These pressures combine to create a powerful force which has an undeniable effect on our relationship.

As the level of pressure on your relationship increases, the more important the Relationship Enablers become.

Argument Graph and ignored Relationship Enablers

Figure 3.1 reveals the correlation between the level of friction between a couple and how arguments reduce the level of friction in the short term. However, in the long term, the overall friction level continues to rise. Unless the cause is resolved, more than likely being a failure to communicate in a way which is consistent with one or more of the Relationship Enablers, their negative influence continues to increase. On the graph, this is represented by circles. Over time, these circles become larger, thereby creating a context for increased negativity. This is why the level of friction gradually follows an upward path. In order to stop this from happening, communicate with your partner in a way which is consistent with all the Relationship Enablers, in the context of Win by Losing.

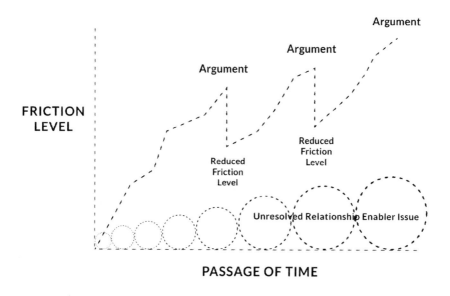

Figure 3.1. Argument graph and unresolved Relationship Enablers

Communicate in a way which is consistent with all five Relationship Enablers and stop those arguments.

If only we could start again: Relationships are easy at first

Why are relationships so much easier at the outset? From a Win by Losing perspective, it's because, in those early days, they exist in a vacuum. When it's just the two of you, things are simple: You meet, chat, and go on a date. What could be simpler than that? You are also in that honeymoon period that happens when you have something new which is, in your eyes, perfect.

You also are in "love," which has biochemical aspects such as oxytocin, the love hormone, altering your thinking when with your partner. Falling in love is partly a biochemical process, but that chemical doesn't last forever. Over time, you form a mutual attachment and other forces start to work their way into your relationship. Your honeymoon, or "blind love," period eventually starts to wear off. Friends, family, work, money, children, running a home, and of equal importance, your own expectations of the relationship are all examples of forces which increasingly make their mark over time.

We are not suggesting these forces are bad. Having children, for example, can be a truly wonderful experience. However, what we are suggesting is that there is no escaping the impact these forces have on your relationship. Adding into the mix your values, beliefs, and behaviors, along with those of your partner, and you have a unique set forces which can act in unexpected ways. One outcome is the almost inevitable development of friction between you, which needs resolution in one way or another. That way is by adopting the Win by Losing method and communicating in a way which is consistent with the five Relationship Enablers.

The happy outcome: Why not win–win?

Arguments are a normal and sometimes healthy part of any relationship. A constructive argument will clear the air and lead to an agreement about how to handle the issue at hand. Both parties walk away happy, knowing the issue has been resolved. It's a win–win. The water which filled the Sink of Negativity, due to the argument, is able to flow away fully. No water from that argument has been left behind.

Unfortunately, this is normally the exception rather than the rule. From a male–female point of view, far more common is a lose–win, or win–lose, outcome, whereby one party is satisfied with the outcome and the other is not. Equally problematic is a lose–lose scenario, when both parties are dissatisfied with the outcome. We don't need to give you examples; it's safe to say this is a universal experience.

The three scenarios—win–lose, lose–win and lose–lose—have two guaranteed longer-term effects on relationships:

1. Water is left behind in the Sink of Negativity (see Chapter 2); and

2. Eventually, there will be another argument about the same or similar issue, which was not resolved the first time around—more likely, one or both parties ran out of the Emotional Energy (see Chapter 2) needed to continue the argument, which is why it came to an end.

However, when one party's emotional batteries are once again fully recharged—perhaps after a good night's sleep—they won't be able to resist the temptation to continue with the battle when the opportunity presents itself.

Normally, whoever is able to recharge their emotional batteries quicker, or whose batteries last longest during the argument will break through and win.

It's not about the facts: The winner is?

In the context of relationships, winning an argument is not about being *right*. Instead, it's purely and simply about being able to win the argument. It could be that the *winner* was right all along, but that's rarely the reason for winning. Who argues on a point of fact, which can easily be proved wrong or right? We have all experienced the most common type of argument where there is a difference of opinion. Neither side can prove objectively that they are right or the other side is conclusively wrong. Arguments don't work that way. This raises the important question of whose emotional batteries last the longest and recharge the quickest.

Your Emotional Energy battery: A reminder why it's so important to you

When in an argument with your partner, communication is normally fueled by the upset or anger you feel at the time. This fuel doesn't last forever and eventually runs out. When this happens, we start to feel less upset or angry and ultimately, no longer feel these negative emotions.

As covered in Chapter 2, with their larger fuel source, developed for a different age in the distant past, women can keep pushing for an outcome most favorable to them due to their greater capacity and faster recharging Emotional Energy batteries. When women keep pushing for their preferred outcome in this way, most men interpret this as *nagging*. This continues until the man no longer cares one way or the other, and eventually gives in, leading to the woman getting her way. This process can be quite fast, taking just a few hours, or can last weeks or even months. No matter how long it takes, the outcome is the normally same. Remember we are focusing on intimate relationships here, rather than any other context such as work or in politics.

Another way of looking at this is in terms of the amount of fuel in a modern commercial aircraft. When the fuel runs out, the airplane will glide to the ground and, in the absence of a safe place to land, will probably crash. With their larger fuel tanks, the typical woman's airplane can travel further and is more likely to reach its intended destination. The destination, of course, is to achieve the desired outcome and win.

Key Points

1. When things start to go wrong in a relationship, you can be sure that you are not communicating in a way which is consistent with one or more of the Relationship Enablers. You need to take action as these matters don't fix themselves.

2. Most of us address the thorniest issues in our relationship during an argument. Instead, raise the issues when both of you are calm

and ready to have a constructive conversation. You can create this context by communicating in a way which is consistent with the five relationship enablers and by adopting the Win by Losing method.

3. Life is tough. Don't make it tougher by thinking you can win all your arguments with your partner. Win by Losing is a much better approach. This will empower you to focus on your ground rules; that is, the things that really matter to you and are not open to discussion, compromise, or negotiation.

4. Winning an argument has nothing to do with being right. It's all about who has the Emotional Energy to keep going and eventually break through and win.

Questions and Answers

Q: What are Relationship Enablers?

A: Relationship Enablers are positive ways of communicating with your partner which lower the Sink of Negativity. You need to ensure your communication is consistent with all five of them. The more pressure on your relationship, the more important these ways of communicating become.

Q: How many Relationship Enablers are there and what are they?

A: There are five Relationship Enablers which are:

1. **I won't back down: Enforce your ground rules** (Chapter 4): Ground Rules are the most important things to you in your life and relationship. Enforcing them ensures they stay in place.

2. **Make every conversation matter: Listening with Intent** (Chapter 5): A way of listening to your partner which encourages effective communication.

3. **We're in this together: Common Purpose** (Chapter 6): Understanding why you are in a relationship together to ensure you both achieve the outcomes you desire.

4. **Just accept it: Acceptance of what we can and cannot change** (Chapter 7): No matter how much you love your partner, you can't change her. Change can only come from within you.

5. **Say what you mean: Straight Talking** (Chapter 8): Saying what's really on your mind in a calm and constructive manner.

Q: Why do Relationship Enablers matter?

A: They matter because you need to communicate in a positive way with your partner to lower the water level in the Sink of Negativity, which in turn, creates the context for a happy relationship. Adopting the Win by Losing method isn't enough.

Q: Are you saying I'm unlikely to be in a happy relationship unless I communicate in a way which is consistent with the Relationship Enablers?

A: Yes, you are much more likely to be in a happy relationship where you adopt the Win by Losing method and communicate in a way which is consistent with the five Relationship Enablers.

Q: Why are relationships so much simpler when couples first meet?

A: When couples first meet, their relationship exists in a vacuum. Over time, pressure is applied from a variety of sources, including family, money issues, differences in opinion, values and beliefs, along with the couple's own expectations of the relationship.

Multiple Choice

1. Most arguments can be permanently resolved by:

    a. Making sure you win every time you argue.

    b. Avoiding every disagreement and just doing what you're told.

    c. Breaking up with your partner and never going out with anyone ever again.

    d. Understanding how your communication needs to change in order to become consistent with the five Relationship Enablers.

2. Soon after the next argument takes place you should:

    a. Keep score. You need to win each and every time.

    b. Get yourself ready for the next argument. It's all in the preparation.

    c. Think about the underlying cause. At the appropriate time, speak with your partner about it.

    d. Complain about your partner to your closest friends and family. That'll fix it!

3. You are more likely to be happy in your relationship when:

    a. You adopt the Win by Losing method and communicate in a way which is consistent with the five Relationship Enablers.

    b. You get what you want.

    c. Your partner's mother is kept happy.

    d. You make lots of money and spend it on your partner.

4. If you want a better relationship with your partner, it's all about:

    a. Making sure you win more arguments.

    b. Improving the way you communicate.

    c. Getting in your partner's friends' good books.

    d. Having kids, because that makes life easier.

5. In order to win an argument and get your own way, you need to:

    a. Get your facts right. Winning is all about being correct.

    b. Shout louder than your partner.

c. Limit the number of arguments to enforcing your ground rules (the things which are most important to you) and investing in the Emotional Energy needed to win.

d. Involve your mother. With her help, you'll be a winner!

Take Action

Take some time to answer and act upon these questions.

1. Describe the first few months of your current or previous relationships. Typically, over this time you started off with no internal or external pressures and they slowly built over time.

    • What were the first internal and external pressures which you can recall?

    • How did the relationship change as time went on? Where these changes sudden or did they creep up on you?

    • What effect did these changes have on your relationship and, most importantly, how you communicated? With the power of hindsight and what you have covered so far in this book, how could you have handled these changes in a different way?

2. Write down a list of internal and external pressures on your relationship. An awareness of these is needed if you are to tackle them in a constructive way.

    • If you are single, choose a previous relationship.

    • Ask your partner to write down what she sees as the internal and external pressures on the relationship.

    • Spend a little time comparing your lists. What's similar? What's different?

    • Which pressures are just a part of life and which are self-imposed? Can any of them be removed by the two of you communicating and working together in a better way?

3. Think about and write down common arguments you have with your partner.

   - Are there any underlying themes or issues to these arguments, which act as fuel to keep these arguments reoccurring? Keep those themes in mind when reading the Relationship Enablers in Chapters 4 – 8.

   - If the underlying issues are difficult to determine, keep a diary of your arguments and, in about two weeks, review your diary. The themes should become clear.

What's Next?

In the next chapter we will introduce you to the first Relationship Enabler – I won't back down: Enforce your Ground Rules.

CHAPTER 4

I won't back down: Enforce your Ground Rules

———————————————————

We shall defend our island, whatever the cost may be … we shall never surrender.

WINSTON CHURCHILL, UK PRIME MINISTER, JUNE 4, 1940.

Why read this chapter? What's in it for you?

In this chapter we will cover:

- ► The key to your happiness: Ground Rules as a Relationship Enabler;
- ► A two-way street: Understanding your partner's Ground Rules;
- ► How power works in relationships and what to do about it: Relationship Dynamics in action;
- ► Understanding flexibility in your relationship: Your boundaries;
- ► Its time for us to share with you: Ground Rule examples;
- ► Key Points;
- ► Questions and answers;
- ► Multiple Choice;
- ► Take Action;
- ► What's Next?

Let's make a start: Introduction

I won't back down: Enforce your Ground Rules is our first Relationship Enabler.

Ground rules are those things which are most important to you in your relationship and in your life. Rather than a long and unobtainable wish list, it's a short list of those things which really matter to you.

Another way of describing ground rules is as *boundaries*—unwritten lines in the sand which your partner must not cross. Whether we talk about *ground rules* or *boundaries* in relationships we mean the same thing. Over a period of time, ground rules will be challenged by your partner, consciously or unconsciously. This is either due to outside forces acting on your relationship (as discussed in Chapter 2), or because your partner decides she wants to change something in the relationship, or something about you, which requires breaking one of your ground rules or crossing one of your boundaries.

As explained in Chapter 2, most people have a built-in understanding and appreciation of fairness. Ground rules must be fair and reasonable – they should never be used as an excuse to control your partner.

Ground rules must never force your partner to do something she doesn't want to do. It's unfair, unreasonable and will fill your partner's Sink of Negativity.

As long as your ground rules are fair and reasonable, it doesn't matter what your partner wants you to do or how they would prefer to communicate with you. These are your ground rules. They are not open to discussion, compromise, or negotiation.

We've sort of been here before: Ground Rules as a Relationship Enabler

We have already discussed ground rules, so why are they also treated as a Relationship Enabler? In Chapter 2 we covered the importance of preserving your Emotional Energy for the enforcement of your ground rules; that is, those things which really matter to you. That was a simplified version of what ground rules are really about. In this chapter, we will go into more detail.

Your partner is not a mind-reader and you need to communicate your ground rules to her—and we don't mean during an argument. This might seem obvious, but have you ever talked to her about what your ground rules actually are? Before you do this, however, do *you* know what they are? Have you ever stopped to think about them? **Stop** and write them down now.

At the beginning of Chapter 1 we asked you to stop and think about what's important to you. Now that we are discussing ground rules, the question is, "What's most important to you about your relationship and in your life right now?" Equally important, especially in the context of Win by Losing, what are your partner's ground rules? Do you know? Does she know? If not, you both need to find out.

When we stop to think about it, how many of us understand our partner's ground rules? Perhaps this goes some way to explain why separation and divorce rates are high.

If you know your partner extremely well, you could probably guess, but that's not the same as talking to her about them in a constructive way. It's the difference between your boss guessing what your motivations are at work and actually asking you. The same is true of ground rules. Guessing your partner's ground rules is never the same as asking about them.

Most of us have actually communicated our ground rules in an indirect way during arguments, but that doesn't count!

Only when ground rules are discussed in a calm and rational way will they be understood by your partner. When understood, they will they have an effect on the way your partner communicates with you.

Look both ways: A two-way street

It's not enough simply to communicate your ground rules to your partner. She will only respect them, and therefore modify her communication to take them into account, when:

- She respects you; and

- You respect her ground rules too.

Respect is a two-way street. It's earned not bought, and it is based on what we know about that person, how they behave toward us and others, how that person communicates with us and how we interpret that communication.

Ground rules are a two-way street. You can't expect your partner to respect your rules if you don't do exactly the same where her ground rules are concerned.

If you don't respect your partner and her ground rules you can't expect respect in return. Do you respect your partner's ground rules? Do you even know what they are?

Perhaps your partner has ground rules which relate to sharing household chores. If you have kids, she almost certainly has one or two ground rules about looking after them. Do you know what they are? What about her friends and family? We are sure she has ground rules about them too.

You should have only a few important ground rules and let everything else go. An important reason for having only a few ground rules rather than a long list is because that's exactly what we would expect from our partners. If you have a long and complex list, expect to receive something equally difficult to live with. On the other hand, if you have only a handful of ground rules, then it's reasonable to expect only a handful from your partner. As they say, "What's good for the goose is good for the gander."

Ground Rules: Not a long list of rules

Ground rules are those things which are most important to you in your life and in your relationship. It's *not* a list of rules. The same should apply to your partner's ground rules too. They should be limited to those things which are most important to her.

We aren't suggesting you have to keep a long list of your partner's ground rules and review them on a daily basis. Your ground rules are not the same as a shopping list as they will be limited to just a handful of topics. Respecting your partner's ground rules shouldn't be a problem for you. She is, after all, your partner! If respecting her ground rules does turn out to be a nightmare, then you need to ask yourself if you are with the right person. Win by Losing. The choice is yours.

Ground rules are the most important things in your life and your relationship. This is the same for your partner. Find out what they are and take action. Respect her ground rules and expect her to respect yours. It's the basis for a happy relationship, especially in the context of Win by Losing.

Example

Let's say you play the guitar at a club every Thursday. This has been in place for many years prior to meeting your partner and is therefore accepted as the norm from the outset. It is the normal way of things. This means that if your partner has plans for a Thursday and you say that you can't make it because you have your evening out at the club, your partner agrees and accepts this as the status quo.

One day, your partner raises this as an issue. Her parents would like to take you both out and have booked a restaurant for a Thursday. **What do you do?** As the Win by Losing method is based on enforcing your ground rules (it is, after all, the "win"), you must use your Emotional Energy to do exactly that—enforce your ground rule. As our method ensures you do not waste your Emotional Energy on unnecessary arguments, you will have enough Emotional Energy to win this argument.

Agreeing to the Thursday dinner on the condition it's a one-off is, in our view, not a fair compromise. If you go ahead and agree, before you know it an equally convincing reason for missing another Thursday night out will find its way to you. You have to know when to hold your ground.

Of course, life is unpredictable and every rule has an exception, including this one. There needs to be a sufficiently watertight one-off reason for allowing your ground rules to be breached, such as a death in the family resulting in a funeral taking place on a Thursday. That represents an acceptable one-off exception.

Returning to the example, your partner's parents will have to change the booking to another day. Enforcing your ground rules can be tough. You must stand your ground on the things which really matter to you. You have to have the courage to take some heat when standing your ground. When your partner sees that you won't back down, she will be less likely to challenge or disrespect your ground rule. When you stop to think about it, you will be surprised how few grounds rules you have: Possibly just three or four, so you must enforce them. If you don't, you will slowly lose your identity and that will ultimately destroy the relationship, as it will create a power imbalance between you which will not be sustainable in the longer term.

It's not just about you: Your partner's Ground Rules

Understanding your partner's ground rules is an effective way of being able to understand, and possibly even predict, the way she communicates with you. Is there something you do or don't do which results in a reaction which is way over the top and disproportionate? If so, you may have come up against one of your partner's ground rules.

As each of us have different ground rules, what's most important to you isn't necessarily important to her.

The opposite also applies where something is unimportant to you—for example, not tidying up, leaving dishes in the sink, leaving clothes on the floor, or coming home drunk—could be major ground rule issues for your partner. It depends what's most important to her.

You can't expect your partner to respect your ground rules if you don't respect hers.

Open your mind: If you don't ask, you'll never know

With this in mind, it's useful to develop an understanding of each other's ground rules. The answer to the question, "What are the most important things about our relationship to you?" is a good start.

Your partner also needs to understand your ground rules too. If she loves and respects you, she won't want to cross them. Investing time in developing a shared understanding of ground rules can go a long way toward resolving differences and unnecessary bad feelings between you.

What is power in a relationship any-way? Relationship dynamics

Power in a relationship can be measured in the same way as keeping score during a tennis match. Each time someone gets their way, they get a point. The person who gets their way the most that day wins the game. The more games you win, the more power that person has in the relationship. There has to be a winner at the end of every day. Someone gets their way and the other party loses out. There is a winner and a loser each time. Life is tough; that's how it works.

Or is it? Is that really the right way of looking at power in your relationship? Is it like playing tennis? Does there have to be a winner and a loser? You don't need to play *against* your partner. Instead of tennis, why not rowing? The two of you could be in the same boat, rowing in the same direction as hard as you can, with your opponent being life's many pressures and challenges. There isn't a winner or a loser, just a solution, no matter how large or small.

It's not a question of winning a point. It's a question of resolving the issue together.

Consider the saying in the military, "No man left behind." When you base your communication and problem-solving on winning *and* losing, someone is always left behind. But when you are in a partnership, you are both rowing and working together to go in the same direction, finding a solution as a team.

Row together, play together, love together or ... play tennis, score points, live alone. Either way, it's your joint choice.

Of course, sometimes the game becomes tennis when you must enforce your ground rules. When this happens, you really do need to win.

Playing to win the ground rule point is not the same as playing to win each and every point.

That, in fact, is why we say that you should be clear that those few ground rules you decide to enforce must be the ones that matter the most to you. Those are the points which matter—the points you need to win. For everything else, don't sweat the small stuff. For 80 percent of the time, rowing together leads to far happier, longer-lasting and intimate relationships. See the latter part of Chapter 2 for details on what to do if you are with someone who falls into the other 20 percent category and seeks to dominate at every opportunity.

Focus on what really matters: Forget the small stuff

As far as Win by Losing is concerned, don't worry or argue about *the small stuff*. Your partner wants patterned cushions, but you don't like them? Just let it go. She will get them one way or another anyway.

Your partner gives you a list of things to do? Just get them done. You will eventually go through the list in any event, so why allow it to become a source of friction and ultimately her victory? Remember the Zero-Sum Game in Chapter 2?

Your partner wants to have her parents over for dinner, but you don't like them? Agree with her and deal with it.

Your partner wants a city holiday, but you want to spend your time on the beach? Enjoy the city!

It's about the time you spend together, not where you spend that time.

Your partner is breaking a clearly communicated ground rule? Face it head on. You don't have many of them so make them count, just as in Tom Petty's and Jeff Lynne's song, "I Won't Back Down."

Contrary to what your partner might say at the time, she will ultimately respect you for standing your ground on the things which matter most to you. Enforcing your ground rules ensures the balance of power remains sustainable in the long term.

Don't back down if your partner breaks one of your ground rules.

You must decide for yourself what your ground rules are and why they are important to you. This is a conscious decision on your part. All too often men drift into arguments with their partners. Pick them wisely and make them count. If we look at arguments in terms of playing a game, then when enforcing your ground rules, you must play to win.

Once you've started to enforce a ground rule in relation to a specific issue, never let it go. In this way, Win by Losing will work for you and provide you with Emotional Energy when you need it most.

It's about being in an effective and happy relationship, rather than being told what to do about everything which is important to you. Your communication must be predictable and consistent: If you say this is the rule, you must enforce it each and every time (except when you don't… nobody said this was easy).

Say it, mean it, own it: Consistency matters

Let's set aside the exceptional one-off life event, when encroachment onto a ground rule is allowed; for example, your weekly Wednesday evening out with friends or your regular trips to the gym that week are cancelled because your partner's grandma dies. Life is full of surprises and we need to be sufficiently flexible and supportive when needed.

However, giving in just once (for a reason unrelated to an extreme life event) suggests to your partner that the ground rule was not that important to you after all. This may be a short-term solution if you are experiencing pressure to break the ground rule, but in the longer term this is something you will live to regret. Equally, the inconsistent enforcement of your ground rules is not fair on your partner.

She needs to know where she stands on those things which matter to you the most.

She may not like it at the time, but in the long term she will accept your ground rules and respect you for enforcing them. This is one of the reasons why you must keep the number of ground rules to a minimum. It's not possible to enforce a long list of ground rules: Identify the things which are the most important to you and make a conscious decision to let the rest go, then you will find you can Win by Losing. Of course, all of this also applies to you where your partner's ground rules are concerned. Mutual respect can only work both ways.

Although some arguments are inevitable, enforcing your ground rules does not necessarily mean having to argue with your partner. You don't always have to *fight* to enforce them. Highlighting the mutual benefits of your preferred course of action or ground rule can go a long way to resolving this issue. Perhaps you can find a compromise where you, for example, spend Thursday nights with your friends on the basis that you look after the kids, if you have them, on a Friday so she can see her friends. We all need time apart. It brings us closer together as it provides fresh perspectives, as well as topics and ideas to talk about and share when together. It's important to note, however, that the compromise in no way enables your partner to violate your ground rule.

All around you: Your boundaries

Figure 4.1 shows the relative importance of our boundaries. Those closest to us are inflexible as they are our most important boundaries—often, they are closely aligned with our identity as a person. Those further away become less important and we can be more flexible in terms of their enforcement.

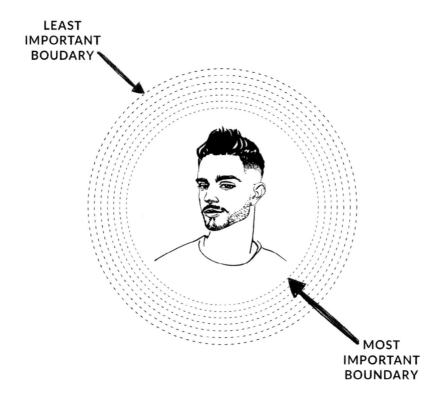

Figure 4.1. Your Boundaries

Clearly, you should understand your own boundaries and their relative levels of flexibility. Ask yourself, "What's most important to me where this relationship and my life is concerned?"

Your answers may provide you with your boundaries. If the answer doesn't, you should ask the follow-up question, "And what's important to me about that?" This will eventually reveal the boundary.

Write them down and rank them to ascertain their relative importance. Make sure you focus on the top three or four, no more than that. Talk to your partner about them to ensure she understands which are the most important. You can't expect her to respect them when she doesn't even know what they are. Women may have impressive amounts of Emotional Energy, but they are useless at mind-reading.

My closest boundaries are who I am. Don't mess with them!

Just like your boundaries, your partner's most important boundaries are the least flexible to her. Understanding your partner's boundaries can be a powerful way of understanding more clearly why she communicates with you in the way she does. Don't try to change your partner's most important boundaries as those are the ones closest to her, and it's highly unlikely she will be able to change them for you. People don't change, no matter how much we love them. She can't change for you, in the same way as you can't change for her.

Remember, her most important boundaries are the least flexible.

When our worlds collide: Clash of the ground rules

Returning to ground rules: What happens if your most important ground rules come into conflict with hers? That's a tricky one! Either you are fundamentally incompatible or you will adopt the Win by Losing method, which means putting her most important ground rules first.

> *Don't try to fight your partner's ground rules. They are probably part of who she is as a person.*

Trying to change your partner's ground rules is a losing battle and your attempts to win the battle will, in the long run, fill the Sink of Negativity, in which case your relationship will end anyway. Under these circumstances, you need to ensure her ground rules come first as any other approach will quickly deplete your Emotional Energy.

Rule number one: Rules are meant to be broken

Although we have said you should enforce your ground rules no matter what, there are always exceptions. As they say, rules are meant to be broken.

Consider the example of Louise and Peter who have been married for fifteen years. Throughout that time Peter's friend Tom has joined them every Sunday for dinner. Come rain or shine, Tom appears at Peter's front door at 6.00 p.m., has dinner with Peter and his family, then they watch TV together or go out for drinks. Peter's kids have become so used to Tom coming over, they don't even regard him as a guest. Sunday evenings are not Sunday evenings without Tom sitting at the dinner table, catching up with them on the events of the week.

As the years go by, Peter and Tom find it increasingly difficult to maintain this long-standing arrangement. Life just keeps getting in the way.

One day, Louise informs Peter that their plans for dinner on Sunday have changed: One of Louise's parents' best friends has passed away and the funeral followed by prayers will be happening on Sunday.

"My parents are so upset. I think we should spend the day with them."

"Do I really have to go? I didn't even meet this friend of your parents. Tom's coming over and we were planning to go out for drinks."

"It's up to you. Whatever you decide is fine with me."

"Well, in that case, I'd rather not go, thanks."

"Fair enough" said Louise as she left the room. Peter thought that was the end of the conversation.

Perhaps predictably Louise reappeared several minutes later, "I've decided to go over to my parents' anyway. They need my support, but I really don't know what I'm going to say about you not being there. You know how much they like to see you. They will be so disappointed you weren't able to support them."

"Fine, I'll go with you," Peter says wisely.

This an example of a time for Peter to adopt our approach and Win by Losing. Even though this meant Tom couldn't come over that Sunday, Peter knew this would be an exception and wouldn't fundamentally change this long-established ground rule.

Sometimes you need to be flexible under these circumstances. It's a judgment you need to make. In Peter's case, the alternative was to flatly refuse to go, which would have been met with a heavy price to pay, with interest, over a relatively long period of time. It would have unnecessarily raised the Sink of Negativity's water level. Moreover it almost certainly would have caused entirely avoidable friction in the future, leading to wasted Emotional Energy as Peter pointlessly argued his case for not joining Louise and her parents.

It's okay to give a rare exception to a ground rule.
You will survive and your rule will too!

Your ground rules don't need to be a dry list of what's most important to you in your relationship and in your life right now. You can personalize them by including something about you, your thoughts and your personality. Take a look at one of your authors and his wife's ground rules below for examples of what we mean.

David and Claire's ground rules

So, what are our ground rules? The question isn't easy to answer and it really did require us to stop and think. When thinking about my ground rules, my mind focused on times where I'd had arguments with girlfriends over the years, all the way to relatively recent times with my wife. Yes, that's right, even one of the authors of this book has arguments: Some are to enforce my ground rules, and others are because I'm just as imperfect as everyone else. We are, after all, only human.

Thinking about times where I really flew off the handle or completely overacted to a situation helped me to identify my ground rules. Perhaps that's not the most positive approach but we don't think about our ground rules when everything is happy and rosy in our relationship.

My ground rules are as follows:

1. Be straight, always tell the truth, and don't play psychological games with me.

2. I need about an hour to myself once every few days: Watching TV, listening to music, tidying up, or just doing some paperwork. Leave me alone during this time.

3. If I'm quiet, I'm thinking. Let me be. It won't take long and I'll be back soon enough.

4. There are always things to do. Just write them in a list and leave them to me. I don't need reminding and will get them done over the next few weeks. If you forget to put them on the list, don't complain if I don't do them.

Claire appreciates and respects these ground rules implicitly, in a way previous girlfriends didn't. That's probably why we have been happily married for over twenty-two years!

What about Claire's ground rules? After some discussion, we established her ground rules were as follows:

1. Always keep to my plan of action. If it doesn't happen the way I planned, something has gone wrong and I find that stressful.

2. My home must be clean and tidy. I can't think straight in a messy environment.

3. Meals must only be eaten at the kitchen table and without mobile phones present.

4. I love lists and need to know you care about getting these things done. There's nothing better than a list with ticks against every item.

Unsurprisingly our ground rules go well together. Perhaps that's one of the secrets of a long and happy marriage.

Key Points

1. Your ground rules are metaphorical lines in the sand which your partner must not cross. Unless they clash with your partner's ground rules, they are not open to discussion, compromise, or negotiation.

2. You are responsible for communicating your ground rules clearly to your partner. Equally, you are responsible for ascertaining and respecting your partner's ground rules. She has the same responsibility too.

3. You should have not more than a handful of ground rules. If you have to write them down to remember them, you have too many.

4. It's a joint decision whether to play tennis or row together.

Questions and Answers

Q: What are ground rules?

A: Your ground rules are those things which are most important to you. Rather than a long and unobtainable wish list, it's a short list of those things which really matter to you. They are lines in the sand which your partner must not cross. Your partner has ground rules too being those things which are most important to her. They are lines in the sand which you must not cross.

Q: Why should ground rules matter to me?

A: This is the "Win" in Win by Losing. These are the things which are fundamental to your being happy in your relationship.

Q: Who decides my ground rules?

A: You do. They are the things in your life and relationship which are most important to you. You may have ground rules concerning having a hobby, time to yourself, or time with your friends.

Q: Does my partner have ground rules too?

A: Yes, she does. Her ground rules are as important to her as your ground rules are to you.

Q: How to I find out my partner's ground rules?

A: Ask her, "What's most important to you about our relationship and in your life right now?" If her answer doesn't seem to be a ground rule, ask, "What's important to you about that?" You may have to ask this last question a few times, but you will eventually discover one of her ground rules.

Q: If one of my ground rules changes over time, should I talk to my partner about that?

A: Yes, women are many things, but we have never met one who can read minds.

Q: What happens if my partner breaks one of the ground rules which I have discussed with her?

A: Bring this up in a calm and rational manner right away. Explain that breaking your ground rule is not acceptable and ask her not to do it again. Make it clear this is a matter of respecting your ground rules as you respect hers. Don't go along with doing something, or not doing something, which will break your ground rules. Make a stand and stick to it!

Q: So, the more ground rules I have the better, right?

A: Wrong. You should keep your ground rules to no more than a handful. In fact, the fewer the better.

Q: What do tennis and rowing have to do with Win by Losing?

A: When things get tough between you or in life, for whatever reason, and the pressure starts to build on either of you, rather than trying to score points against each other and win (as in tennis), work together to find a solution (as with rowing). Save your Emotional Energy and only play tennis when you must win; that is, one of your clearly communicated and consistently applied ground rules is under threat.

Q: What happens if my partner isn't interested in my ground rules?

A: If you are keeping to the Win by Losing method and respecting your partner's ground rules, and she is still not interested in yours, this means she doesn't respect you and is treating you like a doormat. That's when Win by Losing becomes Win by Leaving. Nobody needs to put up with nonsense like that, including you.

Q: How do I know if one of us has more power than the other?

A: One of you having **control** over the other means that there is an imbalance of power. That's unhealthy as in the long term it will fill the Sink of Negativity. Nobody likes to be controlled by someone else.

Q: If there is an imbalance of power, how can this be resolved?

A: By respecting each other's ground rules.

Multiple Choice

1. Ground rules are:

    a. Available in your local library. Everyone has the same ones.

    b. Lines in the sand which your partner must not cross.

    c. Too complicated to bother with.

    d. Only important when married.

2. Your partner's ground rules are:

    a. Of no importance to you.

    b. Secret. You shouldn't share this personal information.

    c. Available on your partner's favorite social media site.

    d. As important to her as your ground rules are important to you.

3. When your partner seems to enjoy breaking your clearly communicated ground rules, even though you are following the Win by Losing method and communicating in a way which is consistent with all five Relationship Enablers, you should:

    a. Tell her that doesn't matter. It's fun being a doormat.

    b. Have an affair. Your partner will almost certainly find out about it and these things always end well.

    c. Take the time to discuss your concerns with your partner in a calm and well thought-out way. Explain why your ground rules are important to you, just as her ground rules are important to her. State that you understand and respect her ground rules, so you expect her to respect yours. That's what people who are in an intimate relationship, and who trust each other, do.

d. Keep this to yourself and become increasingly frustrated until you end the relationship when your Sink of Negativity overflows.

4. It's possible to identify where there's an imbalance of power in your relationship when:

a. You earn a good salary, but your partner earns more than you.

b. You are able to control your partner so she does what you want her to do. It doesn't matter whether or not she agrees. Alternatively, your partner is able to control you, so you do what she wants you to do.

c. Your partner gives you lists of things to do every weekend.

d. It doesn't matter. This has no effect on your relationship.

Take Action

Take some time to answer and act upon these questions.

1. Write down your ground rules.

- Are they fair, reasonable, simple to understand, and few in number?

- Have you discussed your ground rules with anyone before?

- What changes, if any, need to be made to the way you communicate in your relationship so these ground rules are respected by your partner?

2. How well do you enforce your ground rules?

- Do you preserve all your Emotional Energy for the enforcement of your ground rules?

- When you do have to enforce your ground rules, do you remind your partner of what they are and explain why they are important to you? People rarely remember and act upon what we say to them when we shout and blame!

3. If your partner is to respect your ground rules, how do you respect hers? Respect is a two-way street and you need to look both ways.

    *   What are your partner's ground rules?

    *   Explain to your partner what ground rules are and ask her to think about hers. The starting point is to ask, "What's most important to you about our relationship and in your life right now?" If the answer isn't a ground rule, ask, "What's important to you about that?" You may need to ask the latter question a number of times to discover each of her ground rules. Give your partner some time to think about her ground rules. She probably hasn't thought about this before.

    *   When you know your partner's ground rules, how will you respect them?

    *   Write down examples when you have respected your partner's ground rules.

    *   Write down examples when you did not respect your partner's ground rules and describe what happened. Be honest with yourself.

4. How does your partner enforce her ground rules?

    *   If you know your partner's ground rules, does she still have to enforce them? If so, why?

    *   Have you ever broken one of your partner's ground rules because she broke one of yours? What was the outcome of this way of communicating? Did it lower the Sink of Negativity and leave you both happy and content? If you feel it's relevant, discuss a better way of communicating.

5. Does your partner know your ground rules?

- Have you talked about your ground rules in a calm and constructive way?

- Have you listened to her concerns and ensured your ground rules are fair, reasonable and few in number? You shouldn't have a never-ending wish list!

- Does your partner respect your ground rules? If not, why not? Do you respect hers?

6. How does Win by Losing empower you to enforce your ground rules?

    - How much Emotional Energy do you have compared to your partner? Life's tough—be honest.

    - Describe how having a lower water level in the Sink of Negativity, fewer disagreements and less friction/stress between you affect the way you communicate together.

    - In what way are you better able to enforce your ground rules when adopting the Win by Losing method?

7. If one of your ground rules has changed, have you informed your partner?

    - Have you thought through why your ground rule has changed and how this will affect your partner?

    - If you were on the receiving end of your ground rule change, what questions and concerns might you have?

    - When is the best time to raise your change of ground rule with your partner? Probably not, for example, after she's had a long and challenging day at work.

8. What's the difference between playing tennis against each other and rowing together?

    - How do you communicate with your partner? Do you play tennis or row together? Write down examples of both.

- If you play tennis against each other, why is this the case? Does it have to be this way? Adopting the Win by Losing method will lower the Sink of Negativity which, in turn, creates the context for rowing together. Be patient as change takes time.

- Write down examples of when you rowed together rather than played tennis against each other. Talk to your partner about this and acknowledge these successes together.

9. If you must play tennis in order to enforce your ground rules, do you win?

   - If not, is your list of ground rules sufficiently short? Have you adopted the Win by Losing method for everything else?

10. Is there a healthy balance of power between you?

    - Do you have control over your partner? Does she have control over you?

    - Are you able to describe each other's ground rules?

    - Do you understand and respect each other's ground rules in a consistent manner? Have you ever talked about this with your partner?

What's Next?

In the next chapter we will introduce you to the 2nd Relationship Enabler – Make every conversation matter: Listening with Intent, which describes how you can listen with intent so that every conversation matters!

CHAPTER 5

Make every conversation matter: Listening with Intent

Most people do not listen with the intent to understand;
they listen with the intent to reply.

STEPHEN R. COVEY, *THE 7 HABITS OF HIGHLY EFFECTIVE PEOPLE*

Why read this chapter? What's in it for you?

In this chapter we will cover:

- ► Getting it right: How to listen in an effective way;

- ► Understanding, opinion and agreement: Discover the important differences;

- ► Questions and statements: How to distinguish between asking and telling;

- ► Not in the mood to chat? Handling this common issue in a construcive way;

- ► Quality time: How to make it count;

- ► Practice mnemonic;

- ► Key Points;

- ► Questions and Answers;

- ► Multiple Choice;

- ► Take Action;
- ► What's Next?

Let's make a start: Introduction

Make every conversation matter: Listening with intent is our 2nd Relationship Enabler.

We have all had the experience of listening to a boring person drone on about something in which we have no interest. Their voice phases out slowly and our own thoughts consume all our attention. Sometimes we don't even know they have stopped talking, which can be a little embarrassing.

Listening with intent is the opposite. We hear every word the other person says and our own voice in our head manages to keep quiet for long enough to process properly what they are saying. This isn't easy for everyone, but is extremely important in the context of Win by Losing.

Listen with intent: Shut up, hear it all and process it!

Listening with intent can be broken down into two simple parts:

1. listening actively to what our partner is saying to us; and

2. providing feedback to our partner to ensure she is aware that we have listened to what she has said.

The second part is often missed and women are left unsure of whether we have heard what they said to us. A likely consequence of this is that, several minutes or possibly hours later, your partner then repeats herself, assuming that you didn't hear her the first time. Repeating back to your partner a brief summary what she did say is a powerful way of making her aware that you did hear what she had to say.

Not just background noise: Listen carefully

Consider these scenarios:

Scenario 1

"Over the weekend we're seeing our friends Peter and Jane. It's been such a long time since we saw them last. I wonder if they've had their lounge redecorated. We should take a nice bottle of wine when we go over to theirs."

"Hmm. Okay."

Scenario 2

"Over the weekend we're seeing our friends Peter and Jane. It's been such a long time since we saw them last. I wonder if they've had their lounge redecorated. We should to take a nice bottle of wine when we go over to theirs."

"Yes, it'll be great to see Peter and Jane. They'll like a bottle of wine."

Let's face it, Scenario 1 is tempting. Unfortunately, it doesn't make it clear to our partner that we have heard what she said. One consequence is that, soon afterwards your partner may tell you the same thing all over again. That's extremely annoying and will sound as if she's nagging you. If you have ever experienced being nagged in this way, now you know why—it's because your partner is not convinced that you heard and processed what she said. By listening with intent and acknowledging what was said, you can avoid this annoyance and improve communication between the two of you.

Scenario 3

You can add to the Scenario 2 response by responding at a higher level, to show not only that you heard, but also that you were thinking about her idea. For instance:

"Are you sure they'll want wine? I thought last time we saw them Jane said to you that she thought Peter was drinking too much. Maybe we should get a box of chocolates. What do you think?"

Or if Peter does not have a drinking problem you could say,

"Do you think a red wine or a white wine would be better? Maybe find out what she's cooking?"

Scenario 1, with the response of "Hmm. Okay," is typical when a man comes home from a busy day at work, but it's not the type of response a woman needs to hear. Not *wants* to hear, but *needs* to hear. There's an important difference. Listening with intent demonstrates that you have heard what she said and, equally important, that *what she says matters to you*.

Scenario 3 shows that you not only heard her but that you have thought about it and come up with a suggestion that she may not have considered.

Your partner needs to know you have heard and processed what she said—not what you *think* she meant, but what she *actually* meant. If her meaning is not clear, ask her to clarify. Showing you understand is an important way of demonstrating to her that *what she says matters to you*.

Listen with intent: It's important she knows you genuinely care about what she said.

What I'm being asked to do: Understanding, opinion, and agreement

When your partner shares her thoughts with you, she is looking for your understanding, opinion, or agreement. Getting this wrong can have unexpected consequences. In her head, it's clear which one she's after, but from a man's perspective, it can be difficult to get this right.

Generally speaking, if your partner shares information with you about something she is upset about, but which has nothing to do with you, she is looking for your understanding. Listen with intent and acknowledge what she has said to you. Acknowledgment is the simple process of summarizing and saying back what you have heard. Generally, under these circumstances, you don't need to offer your opinion unless she asks for it.

Women can understandably become upset when they tell their partner about an issue and he immediately jumps in with a solution. Most of the time she just wants him to listen to her and empathize, like her girlfriends do. They don't want their partner to find a solution to the issue. It's about feelings not solutions. They know the best solution already.

There are times when your partner needs your understanding, not necessarily your opinion or agreement.

How do you know when your partner is looking for your opinion and when she is looking for agreement? The answer lies in the way she asks the question. If she provides you with *her* opinion in her question, then she's normally looking for agreement. On the other hand, if she makes no reference to her own preferred course of action in the question, then she's looking for *your opinion*.

We have included some examples below of when your partner is more likely to be looking for your understanding, your opinion, or your agreement. What works for one woman may not work for another. It's your relationship so you need to develop a good understanding of what your partner is communicating, and what she wants from you. These examples therefore won't apply to everyone.

Examples

1. **Understanding**

   - "I'm so upset about what happened at work today. My boss was rude to me."

   - "I thought Jane was my best friend, but she really upset me today."

   - "My mother won't drop it. She mentions it to me every time I speak to her."

2. **Opinion**

- "I'm so upset about what happened at work today. My boss was so rude to me. Do you think I should talk to her about it?"

- "I thought Jane was my best friend, but she really upset me today. She said I hadn't reached my full potential just because I didn't go to university. Is that true?"

- "My mother won't drop it. She mentions it to me every time I speak to her. What do you think I should say to her about that?"

3. **Agreement**

- "I'm so upset about what happened at work today. My boss was so rude to me. I'm going to tell him that's completely unacceptable behavior. Do you think that's a good idea?"

- "I thought Jane was my best friend, but she really upset me today. She said I hadn't reached my full potential just because I didn't go to university. The next time I speak to her I'm going to tell her that's complete nonsense. What do you think?"

- "My mother won't drop it. She mentions it to me every time I speak to her. I'm going to tell her enough is enough. Do you agree?"

When it's unclear if your partner actually wants you to agree with her opinion or is looking for your agreement, you can always ask her, "Hold on a minute. Are you asking for my agreement about what you intend to do, or do you want to hear my opinion?"

Telling the difference: Questions and statements

There are times when it can be difficult to figure out the difference between a question and a statement. For example, you partner may ask the classic question, "Do I look good in this?"

Men often mistake this for a question. It isn't a question; it's actually a statement—"Tell me I look great in this."

Therefore, any answer other than, "You look beautiful in that," will not be well received.

Knowing if your partner is asking you a genuine question can be tricky. Examples include:

- "Does the dishwasher need emptying?"

- "Do you think your car needs cleaning?"

- "Do we need to visit your mother over the weekend?"

These may seem like questions, but it's likely they are, in fact, statements; for instance:

- "It's your turn to empty the dishwasher."

- "You need to clean your car."

- "It's time we visited your mother this weekend."

If you assume a question really is a question, and not a statement, you may find your partner's reaction unreasonable or unpredictable!

Unless you are absolutely sure it's a question, there is no harm in asking. "Is that a question or a statement?" If in doubt, and if for some reason you can't check, assume it's a statement rather than a question. You will be surprised how often your partner will agree that what she said was actually a statement rather than a question.

Listening with intent will go some way to developing your ability to ascertain the difference among a question, a statement, a statement disguised as a question and a question disguised as a statement. Nobody said communicating with women was easy!

Applying Listening with Intent: Quality time

It's not unusual for a man to think he is spending **quality time** with his partner, but then be surprised to discover this was not the case. He had thought that just by being there and keeping his partner company this was sufficient. To most women, however, this isn't enough.

Women need to know their partner has listened to what they have said and is actively engaged in the conversation. Only under these circumstances is the time spent together more likely to be perceived as quality time. This explains why sitting in the same room, watching TV, and not listening to what your partner is saying doesn't normally count as quality time. More information about quality time is provided in Chapter 6: We're in this together: Common Purpose.

If you aren't concentrating on what's being said, you're only hearing. When you clear your mind of other thoughts and concentrate on your partner's communication, you are listening. Hearing is done with the ears, listening is done with the brain!

We've all experienced times where we've come home from a long day at work and our partners seem to have lots to say: We start listening, but soon her voice fades into the background. She then stops talking as she's waiting for an answer to a question. That's when we get caught out as we don't know what to say—we didn't hear the question.

So, what do you do about this? The Win by Losing approach is to say it how it is. If you're not going to listen, tell her: "I just need some time to myself. Let's talk about this a little later/after dinner/tomorrow morning." This is a more constructive approach compared to your partner talking and you not listening to what she has to say. It does mean though that when, "little later/after dinner/tomorrow morning" arrives, you must take the time to listen with intent.

Practice makes perfect: "Practice" mnemonic

Listening with intent is probably the most difficult Relationship Enabler to master. Keep this mnemonic in mind as you develop your ability to listen and communicate in this way.

P: *Persevere.* This may be a new skill which takes time for you to develop.

R: *Repeat* a brief summary of what you have just heard to demonstrate the fact you have listened. It means the time you spend together is far more likely to be seen as quality time by your partner.

A: *Allow* time for your partner to say what she needs to say.

C: *Concentrate* on what your partner is saying to you, not on the voice in your head that's wondering what's for dinner, or on TV that evening.

T: *Talking* is the most important way your partner makes sense of her world.

I: *Inexplicable* reactions from women are sometimes to do with men not understanding whether their partner wants their understanding, opinion, or agreement.

C: *Concentrate* on what you are saying to your partner. Are you wasting valuable Emotional Energy on unimportant disagreements?

E: *Everyone* can listen with intent. It's a matter of patience and practice.

Key Points

1. Listening with intent is concerned with listening to what your partner is saying to you (rather than to the voice in your head), and providing brief feedback to ensure she is aware you have listened. In the context of Win by Losing, you must follow both parts for this process to work properly: that is, listen and provide feedback.

2. Listen. Focus. Say. This Relationship Enabler may take time for you to develop. Keep practicing and be patient with yourself.

3. There are times where our partners are looking for our under-standing, opinion, or agreement. It can be difficult to tell the difference. There are important clues in the context and way in which women talk to us, which we can use to distinguish between them. If in doubt, ask.

4. Unless you are listening with intent to what she's saying, the time you spend with your partner doesn't count as quality time as far is she is concerned.

Questions and Answers

Q: What is listening with intent?

A: Listening with intent is where we hear every word our partner says and our own voice in our head keeps quiet for long enough to process what she is saying to us. We then provide a brief summary of what she said back to her.

Q: So, there's no issue with wondering what I'm having for dinner and what's on TV this evening when listening in this way?

A: If you really are listening with intent, you will *only* be thinking about the words your partner is saying to you. Save all your other thoughts for another time.

Q: This way of listening is harder than I thought. Shall I just give up?

A: Never give up. It's a skill which may take you some time to develop. As with everything, the more you practice, the better you will become.

Q: I find what my partner has to say really boring. In this case, does listening with intent really matter?

A: It most certainly does matter. If you find what your partner has to say so boring, why are you are with her in the first place?

Q: How do I listen with intent?

A: There are two parts to this:

1. Listen actively to what your partner is saying to you (rather than to the voice in your head); and

2. Provide brief feedback to ensure she is aware that you have listened.

In the context of Win by Losing, you must follow both parts for this process to work properly.

Q: I'm no mind-reader. How am I supposed to know when my partner is looking for my understanding, my opinion or my agreement?

A: The context and way in which your partner shares her thoughts with you contain important indicators of which outcome she seeks. Alternatively, there's nothing wrong with simply asking her.

Q: Does listening with intent lead to instant and transformative results?

A: No. Nothing works so quickly where changing communication is concerned. It takes time and patience. The best things come to those who wait and persevere!

Multiple Choice

1. Where most men are concerned, the Relationship Enabler of listening with intent is:

    a. Easy. It comes naturally to listen in this way.

    b. Relatively challenging and takes some patience and practice.

    c. Irrelevant. It doesn't matter how you listen to your partner. She always thinks you're wonderful.

    d. Only important when your partner is really annoyed with you.

2. Your partner will know that you're listening with intent because:

    a. You will provide her with brief summaries of what she says to you throughout the conversation.

    b. You'll constantly interrupt her and ensure you discuss more interesting topics, like food and football.

    c. You'll be looking around the room trying to find something less boring to talk about.

    d. You'll start doing something else, like playing with your phone or watching TV.

3. Your partner tells you she is upset about something (that is not to do with you) and you don't know if she wants your agreement or opinion, you should:

    a. Always give your opinion. You know best.

    b. Ask her what she is actually asking. Does she really want to hear your opinion?

    c. Agree with her and ten minutes later tell her you've changed your mind and her idea was nonsense.

    d. It doesn't matter. You weren't listening and have no idea what she was talking about.

4. Your partner asked you if you would like to take the trash out of your car. This means:

    a. You have an option and she won't mind if you say, "No" and continue watching television.

    b. Your partner actually wants to clean out the car herself and is waiting for you to give her a pair of plastic gloves, a mop, and bucket.

    c. You should tell you partner that you don't care what she thinks of the mess in your car. It's got nothing to do with her anyway.

    d. This isn't a question. It's a statement, meaning, "If you want me to go in that car of yours again, clean it up." You can clean it out, pay someone else to clean it out or just leave it as it is.

5. If your partner and her best friend have an argument, the best thing you can do is:

   a. Get involved and give your opinion. You understand the dynamics between women and can solve these things easily.

   b. Arrange a meeting between your partner and her friend. It will be easy to facilitate and you won't get sucked into the disagreement.

   c. Support your partner, but don't try to offer a solution. You don't understand the complex dynamics between your partner and her friend and are unlikely to be in a position to find a solution.

   d. Don't take any interest in supporting your partner. You have much more interesting things to do and nothing to worry about as this approach won't come back to haunt you in the future.

Take Action

It's time to take action and practice what we have covered in this chapter.

Listen, Focus, Say

Put this into practice by remembering three words: Listen, Focus, Say:

- *Listen* to what your partner is saying;

- *Focus* on her words (not the voice inside your head that's wondering what's for dinner); and

- *Say* a brief summary of what she has said back to your partner.

Try it. You will be amazed at the results!

Remember: Listen, Focus, Say.

Exercise: Conversation Feedback

It's easy for us to say, "Just go ahead and listen with intent." It's not so easy to do. It takes time, practice, and patience. Some of our Relationship Enablers are *ready-made*; you are good to go. This one is more difficult to implement. It takes time and effort on your part. There are no shortcuts, so we have some homework for you.

With a friend or your partner ask them to have a conversation with you and share five things about themselves which you may not know. Then provide them with a summary of what they have just said to you.

They then tell you five more things and you repeat those back to them too. They shouldn't just list these for you. That would be too easy and not how conversations normally work. You should be the one asking questions to gain this information.

Next, your friend or partner should tell you about what's been happening in their lives over the last week or so. It doesn't need to be exciting or interesting events, just what's been happening. Listen for 3–5 minutes and summarize this back to them. It's not as easy as it sounds. Variations include: asking your friend or partner about their holiday, childhood, interests, or hobbies. There are always opportunities to practice listening with intent.

Repeat these exercises weekly and you will find your ability to listen with intent quickly improves over time. Whatever happens, and however long it takes to master this Relationship Enabler, your efforts will not go unrewarded.

Listening with intent ensures the time you spend together is seen as quality time by your partner. It will also reduce the instances of misunderstanding and, in time, will make for an easier way of communicating.

By adopting the Win by Losing method, enforcing your clearly communicated ground rules, respecting your partner's ground rules and listening with intent, you will soon notice a transformation in your relationship.

Exercise: Partner Feedback

The way men and women communicate with each other differs quite considerably. Over the next week or so we recommend spending time listening when women talk to each other. You will notice how they can be far more interactive and communicative than men. It's rare for a woman to reply with "Hmm. Okay," so you should avoid it too.

As an exercise, adopt the approach of summarizing back briefly what you hear to your partner. We are certain that you will be surprised how much your communication will improve. Listening with intent is an important Relationship Enabler as it ensures your partner feels that you listen to what she has to say. It also ensures you really *do* listen to what she has says as it's simply not possible to listen in this way and fail to absorb what is being said.

Take some time to answer these questions.

1.   Write down what quality time with your partner means to you.

     •   Your interpretation of quality time may be different from that of your partner. What does it mean to her? How do you know? Have you asked?

     •   Based on **your** interpretation of quality time, give examples of how, when, and where you and your partner have spent quality time together over the past three months.

     •   Based on **your partner's** interpretation of quality time, ask her to give examples of how, when, and where you and her have spent quality time together over the past three months.

     •   Do you spend enough quality time together, based on **both** your interpretations on what constitutes quality time? If yes, that's great. If not, what changes are needed? Does your partner agree?

- Where changes are needed to the amount or type of quality time you spend together, agree a date and time for the two of you to review whether these changes have taken place. If you don't, how will you know that you are spending enough quality time together – according to **both** of you?

2. Do you really listen and care about what your partner has to say?

   - Write down examples of when you have Listened with Intent over the past two weeks.

   - Show your examples to your partner. Does she agree with you? If not, why not?

   - Listening with intent takes time and practice. Over the next two weeks, write down when you have listened in this way, and describe how it affected the way you communicate with your partner. How did listening with intent affect the Sink of Negativity?

3. What women say isn't always what they mean.

   - Do you interpret what your partner says correctly?

   - How do you know? Have you checked?

4. Have you had a long day and are not in the mood to concentrate on what your partner has to say?

   - That's okay. Just be honest and tell her. Agree a time when she will update you on, for example, the day's events and anything else that's on her mind. Make sure you follow up and spend some quality time with her.

   - Write down what happens when you adopt this approach to the way you communicate.

   - Are there ever times when your partner isn't in a frame of mind to talk with you? If so, how do you handle this? If you can ask to delay a conversation for a time that suits you better, then she can too.

What's Next?

In the next chapter we will introduce you to the third Relationship Enabler – We're in this together: Common Purpose. We will cover how to think about **We not Me.**

CHAPTER 6

We're in this together: Common Purpose

Let's not forget it's you **and** me vs. the problem … not you **vs.** me

STEVE MARABOLI, BEHAVIORAL SCIENTIST

Why read this chapter? What's in it for you?

In this chapter we will cover:

- ▶ It's all in the 'why': Finding your common purpose for being together;

- ▶ Affection and intimacy: Understanding the difference and why it matters;

- ▶ Don't just drift apart: How to stay together;

- ▶ Quality time;

- ▶ Key Points;

- ▶ Questions and Answers;

- ▶ Multiple Choice;

- ▶ Take Action;

- ▶ What's Next?

Let's make a start: Introduction

We're in this together: Common Purpose is our 3rd Relationship Enabler.

Small talk: Some people love it and others hate it. Whatever your view, it helps fill in awkward silences and gives us something to say when nothing else comes to mind. One of the key ingredients that differentiates small talk from more meaningful conversation is the *level* of that conversation.

The next time you find yourself in the middle of small talk ask the other person, "What's important to you about that?" This will lift the conversation to a more interesting level, where you can start to have a meaningful conversation and learn something about each other.

For example, you might find yourself talking about pets. The other person says they have a dog and take it for walks every day. If you ask the question, "What's important to you about having a dog?" the reply will shine a light on their thoughts and feelings about having a pet. The conversation has moved into a higher and more meaningful level.

Don't leave it to chance: A lack of understanding

It's common to be in a relationship where we have no understanding about what our partner really wants from the relationship. We tend to assume their wants and needs are the same as ours. Having an agreed common purpose to the relationship removes this as a potential issue. Notice that having a common purpose is not the same as having agreed ground rules.

*A common purpose is concerned with **why you** are together and what **you both want** from the relationship.*

Don't assume your reasons for being in the relationship are the same as your partner's. Although you can probably guess, unless you ask, you will never know for sure. There's no substitute to hearing your partner's purpose for being in a relationship with you, in her own words.

Avoid a common mistake; Don't assume she has the same wants and needs as you.

"I'm off to the ball game," said Peter.

"Really? Why don't you ever spend time with me?" protested Jane.

"What? I have no idea what you mean," spluttered Peter. "I spend time with you every day! We have breakfast together, dinner together, sleep in the same bed together. We went shopping together last weekend."

"Oh, fine then. Just go with your friends and leave me at home!"

Clearly this conversation isn't making any progress and will probably develop into an argument when Peter gets home from the game. Water will be added to the Sink of Negativity, Emotional Energy will be wasted, and no resolution or agreement will come from the inevitable argument.

At a more appropriate time, a constructive question for Peter to ask is, "What's important to you about us spending time together?" This will yield some interesting findings for Peter to understand his partner better.

Jane might, for example, reply, "For me, spending time together is going for a walk in the park or out to a restaurant."

That's not what Peter had assumed and it provides him with a new insight into what his partner wants and values from their relationship.

Ask your partner: "What's important to you about us spending time together?" You may be surprised what you hear. Remember to Listen with Intent!

Based on this information they can schedule time when they go for walks and out to eat. It doesn't matter whether or not these are things Peter wants to do. That's not the point. Like so many of us these days, Peter and

Jane lead busy lives. That said, there is nothing to stop them from scheduling these activities, which makes them more likely to happen. Going for a walk in the park or out to dinner will be an enjoyable experience for both of them. The next time there's a ball game with Peter's friends, Jane's reaction will be to kiss him goodbye and tell him to enjoy the game. Win by Losing. Everyone's a winner!

Two purposes: It's time to ask

You don't need to wait for a problem to arise before learning something new about your partner. At any time, you can ask her: "What's important to you about being in a relationship with me/marriage/having children together?"

Of course, setting some context about having read this book might be needed before asking this type of question. Suddenly blurting it out will leave your partner wondering why you're asking. However, you may be surprised what you learn and how this can help you to better understand her purpose for being in a relationship with you.

When you discover your partner's purpose, the next question to ask is: What's your own purpose? And more importantly: Are the two aligned? Although this is quite a generalization, many men fall in love and stay in a long-term relationship because they were physically attracted to their partner and liked her company. There's nothing wrong with that. However, some simple questions will provide you with insights from your partner, whose thinking will probably be quite different from yours.

Be clear on the differences: Affection and intimacy

There is a song entitled "Always On My Mind," You may have heard the versions recorded by Elvis Presley, released in 1972, or the excellent Pet Shop Boys' version from 1987. The lyrics are about someone who always had loving and positive thoughts about their partner, but failed to communicate this to them. A complete lack of affection caused the relationship to end and only afterwards does he realize his mistake—only when it's too late does he finally tell her how he felt. Sadly, the damage to the relationship has been done and his words of love and appreciation are no longer sufficient to save their relationship. Don't let this happen to you!

When you ask your partner what she wants from your relationship, one of the top items on their list will probably be affection. She'll want you to hold hands or sit and talk with her. She'll want to cuddle on the couch or in bed. That's the sort of thing she will probably say and you need to appreciate this is important to her.

Most women don't think the same way as men. For them, affection is extremely important and a passionate evening together doesn't tell them that you love them. Affection, on the other hand, does.

Affection beats intimacy every time; affection says, "I love you."

What does this mean? Simple, if you want to show your partner how you feel about her, you don't need to spend your hard-earned money buying her gifts. Instead, show her some affection. Equally, don't be surprised if you are in a relationship where there is a lack of affection between you and you wake up one day to realize that levels of intimacy are also low. If you want to improve the level of intimacy between you, start by showing some affection.

Show affection to improve intimacy.

It doesn't have to be this way: Don't just drift apart

"You two were together for fifteen years. Why did you break up? Wasn't there anything you could have done about it?"

"Not really. We just drifted apart."

People don't just drift apart. The main reason for this is the fact that one or both parties didn't get what they wanted from the relationship.

This happens because they lacked an understanding of what each of them wanted from the relationship, and made incorrect assumptions about each other's purpose for being together. Don't let that happen to you. Talk to your partner and ask her.

Make good use of your understanding and don't think you can change her mind about these things. What your partner wants from the relationship is driven by her values and you can forget about changing those— they are here to stay. The same can be said of your wants and needs too. Remember to Listen with Intent and feed back to her a brief summary of what you hear. Make sure you fulfill each other's needs; not just the physical needs but the psychological needs too. For women, it's the latter which are so important. In fact, if her psychological needs aren't fulfilled, you can forget about anything else.

Her values dictate what she wants from the relationship: You can't change those.

A fundamental truth: Your partner can't change for you

This brings us to an interesting point concerned with trying to change your partner if you don't like what they have to say about their purpose of being in a relationship with you.

There is sometimes a misconception that, if the other person loves us enough, they will change for us. Guess what? They think exactly the same thing.

Example

Aaron and Ann have been engaged for three years and are planning to marry soon. They are very happy together, but there is one issue between them which never seems to go away. Aaron lived in Australia until he was fourteen and very much wants to emigrate there with Ann. Unfortunately, Ann has no interest in living in Australia. Her family and friends live in England, which is where she has lived all her life. Although wonderful for a holiday, living in Australia fills her with dread (although we're sure it's a great place to live). It's simply not what she's used to. It's not home.

This thorny topic has been the cause of many arguments since they met. Aaron has become convinced that, if Ann loves him enough, she will eventually come around to his way of thinking and agree to live in Australia with him. He often thinks to himself, *Ann and I get on so well together. We love each other very much. Surely Ann will change her mind for me eventually.* As the months and years have gone by he has found it increasingly difficult to understand why she just won't see things his way.

Ann, on the other hand, is following exactly the same reasoning and can't understand why Aaron still keeps talking about living in Australia. Surely, if he loved her enough, he would change his mind and continue to live in the England.

Interestingly, neither raises this directly with the other. It would be the most difficult of conversations, so both choose to avoid it.

In our opinion, this is a case where each of them has the same ground rule being, 'I want to live in the country of my choice.' For this relationship to succeed, Aaron or Ann will have to let go of this particular ground rule, which might not be possible to do.

Who's right? Who's wrong? It doesn't matter. All that matters here is to understand that people don't change and your partner certainly won't change for you. Don't waste your energy trying to change someone into what you want them to be. Accept them as they are, the way they look, their values, and what's important to them about your relationship. This will stand you in good stead over the years.

Making it count: Quality time together

In Chapter 5 we explained the importance of listening with intent to increase the likelihood of time spent together being interpreted by your partner as **quality time**. However, this isn't the whole story where quality time is concerned.

What's equally important is to appreciate that it's not about what you do together but the fact that you spend time together surrounded by positive energy. It's this positive energy which has the capacity to turn time spent together into quality time. For example, a day out to the park for a picnic lunch will hardly qualify as quality time together if you spend it arguing. It is, of course, the way you communicate which determines whether the time you spend together is perceived by both you and your partner as quality time.

*One of the misconceptions men have is that spending time with their partner is all about the **quantity** of time spent rather than the **quality** of that time.*

For most women it does not matter if you spend an hour or twelve hours together, but *how* you spend that time which it key. You could be watching TV shows in the same room and not conversing. You as a man will likely say to yourself that you spent, for example, three hours with her when you could have been doing something else. She, on the other hand, will wonder why you bothered and will probably think to herself, *He just sits there saying nothing, with that stupid look on his face, acting like he did me a favor.*

Quality time to her is time spent interacting on the communicative and emotional level, making a connection and adding positive energy, reducing the water level in the Sink of Negativity, or making deposits into the relationship account (See Chapter 2). It's like attendance in class versus active participation. The man thinks showing up is enough, whereas the woman will give him an 'F' if he doesn't actively communicate with her.

> *Where your partner is concerned, she wants you to participate actively. Simply being in the same room doesn't count!*

Creating quality time together: Taking an interest

It's far more likely for time spent together to be seen by your partner as quality time when you take an interest in whatever interests her. We're not interested whether it interests you! If you have no interest in what interests your partner, you shouldn't be with her in the first place. Loving her means you care about what she cares about. What's important to her must be (or become) important to you.

> *Women are extremely perceptive: If you're not interested, she will know about it.*

It's your responsibility to take an interest in whatever your partner is interested in. Perhaps she's interested in religion, friends, family, food, art, literature. Whatever interests she has, you need to spend time taking an active interest and talking to her about them. Put your smartphone away and forget about catching up on the football scores. This is quality time with your partner where you can create and develop the common interests in your relationship.

Key Points

1. Developing an understanding of what you and your partner want from your relationship doesn't cost anything and is relatively easy to do. It is a powerful way of improving mutual understanding and removing unnecessary friction between you.

2. Ask your partner, "What's important to you about being in a relationship with me?" If her answer doesn't seem to be what you are looking for ask, "What's important to you about that?"

3. Intimacy and affection may be the same as far as you are concerned, but that's unlikely to be the case for your partner. A happy relationship is the consequence of applying the Win by Losing method, enforcing your ground rules, listening with intent, spending quality time together, and giving plenty of affection.

Questions and Answers

Q: Does it really matter if I don't know what my partner wants from the relationship?

A: Yes. It matters because, in the absence of any other information, you will assume her wants and needs are the same as yours. That almost certainly is not the case and will create unnecessary tension between you.

Q: How do I figure out my partner's purpose for being in a relationship with me?

A: Just ask her, "What's important to you about being in a relationship with me?" If her answer doesn't seem to be what you are looking for ask, "What's important to you about that?"

Q: Just being around my partner is enough to count as quality time together, right?

A: Wrong. It's how you communicate when you are together that determines whether your partner will see it as quality time. If you aren't listening with intent and doing something which interests her, it doesn't count as quality time.

Q: I now know what my partner wants from the relationship and I've given some thought to this as well. The two are different, but does this matter?

A: Not necessarily. As long as they aren't in conflict that's fine.

Q: I've recently confirmed what I have known for a long time: What my partner wants from our relationship is different from, and incompatible, with what I want and need. How can I change her?

A: It's not possible for her to change for you, just as you can't change for her. Change can only come from within you. Talking about these differences normally leads to a constructive way forward. Compromise is a good starting point and, as long as you keep communicating in a calm, open-minded, and rational manner, you will find a constructive solution and a way forward together.

Q: Affection and intimacy are the same thing to me. Does this mean it's also the same for my partner?

A: No. Most women see affection and intimacy as two different things. Being intimate doesn't mean you are being affectionate. This is an important distinction which needs to be appreciated. If you want a higher level of intimacy, a good starting point is to be more affectionate. Examples of being affectionate include holding hands, telling your partner that you love her, and having a cuddle.

Multiple Choice

1. Finding your own and your partner's common purpose is:

    a. Extremely difficult. It takes many hours of dedication and hard work.

    b. Complex and expensive. Only trained psychotherapists are able to ascertain this hard to find information.

    c. Easy and free. All you need to do is to choose the right time, set the context for asking, and ask the right questions.

    d. Irrelevant. It doesn't matter and I don't really care.

2. Women see intimacy and affection as two separate things because:

    a.   They are being deliberately difficult.

    b.   Their mothers told them to make sure the way they communicate is both confusing and unpredictable.

    c.   They are easily confused.

    d.   It's normal for most women to separate these things. This means being intimate doesn't necessarily mean you are being affectionate.

3. If you discover your purpose for being in the relationship is not the same as your partner's:

    a.   Talk about the differences. Are you really incompatible? Is there a way of ensuring both sets of purposes can be achieved? With an open mind and constructive ongoing communication, you will find a way forward together.

    b.   It's a disaster. There's no hope and you should end the relationship.

    c.   You should just ignore the differences and hope it doesn't matter in the longer term.

    d.   You don't care. It's only a short-term relationship anyway.

Take Action

Take some time to answer and act upon these questions.

1. Why are you in a relationship with your partner?

- Write down what you want from your relationship. Don't worry if you're not sure. A good starting point is to ask yourself, "What's the purpose of being in a relationship with my partner? Rank each of the reasons why you are in a relationship from "1" (does not meet my needs) to "10" (meets my needs).

- It may be useful to share this with your partner. Equally it may not! That's up to you. However, if your partner doesn't know there's something wrong, she will probably assume everything is fine. Isn't that what you do?

2. Why is your partner in a relationship with you?

   - What does she want out of it?

   - How do you know? Have you asked her?

   - If possible, share your purpose for being in your relationship and your rating of each purpose together. If this exercise is carried out in a calm and non-blaming manner, it's a great starting point to improving your relationship. However, if there are challenges in your relationship, this task is more likely to be successful if you have finished reading every chapter in this book before embarking on this exercise.

3. Are you both getting what you want from your relationship?

   - Is the purpose of being together the same or different?

   - Where something new is needed, identify the one change which you both agree will make the biggest difference. Focus on that one change and work together to make it happen.

   - When that one thing you have agreed upon is resolved, let a few weeks go by and, if needed, identify one more. You only need to work on one thing at a time. This isn't a race!

4. Has the purpose of being in your relationship changed over time?

   - Over time, our view of life and what we want from it can change. Has yours?

   - If yes, what does this mean about how you communicate and spend time together? What effect has this had on your relationship? Is your partner aware of these changes? She's no mind-reader and won't know about it unless you tell her in a calm, constructive, and forward-looking, solution-focused way (that means you don't say things such as "it's all your fault").

5. Has your partner's purpose changed over time? How do you know? Have you asked her?

    •   If your purpose hasn't changed over the years, don't assume the same applies to your partner.

6. How much affection, as opposed to intimacy, do you show your partner? Are you sure? Have you asked her?

    •   Can you list five times over the past month when you have shown affection rather than intimacy? If you can, show this list to your partner. Does she agree these were examples of affection? If she doesn't agree (which we wouldn't find surprising) then ask her to provide you examples of what she sees as being affectionate. Whatever happens, don't react negatively to what she says to you. If you do, it may create an issue around being affectionate in your relationship and that's not a constructive way forward as it will add to the Sink of Negativity.

What's Next?

In the next chapter you will learn about the 4th Relationship Enabler – Just Accept it: Acceptance of what we can and cannot change.

CHAPTER 7

Just Accept It: Acceptance of What We Can And Cannot Change

Far too many people are looking **for** the right person, instead of trying to **be** the right person.

GLORIA STEINEM, FEMINIST AND POLITICAL ACTIVIST

God, grant me the serenity
to accept the things I cannot change;
courage to change the things I can;
and wisdom to know the difference.

SERENITY PRAYER, REINHOLD NIEBUHR (1892–1971)

Why read this chapter? What's in it for you?

In this chapter we will cover:

- ▶ Just accept it: Accepting the things about your partner you cannot change;

- ▶ Facing up to your reality: Courage to tackle the things you can change;

- ▶ A constructive approach: How to tackle a major area of concern;

- ▶ A wise man: Knowing the difference between what we can and cannot change;

- ▶ Key Points;

- ▶ Questions and Answers;

- ▶ Multiple Choice;

- ▶ Take Action;

- ▶ What's Next?

Let's make a start: Introduction

Acceptance of what we can and cannot change is our 4th Relationship Enabler.

In this chapter we outline how you can create the context for tackling any area of concern you may have about your relationship in an effective way.

The "Serenity Prayer" (see above) applies to so many facets of our lives, including intimate relationships. Understanding and communicating in a way which is consistent with this Relationship Enabler saves us from unnecessary disagreements and arguments which wastes Emotional Energy, that we should be saving for enforcement of our ground rules.

Merriam-Webster defines "wisdom" as, the "ability to discern inner qualities and relationships." The word "serenity" comes from the Latin "*serenus*," meaning "calm or peaceful."

Using the prayer as a structure for this chapter, we have broken it down into three parts as follows:

1. Just accept it: Accepting the things about your partner you cannot change.

2. Facing up to your reality: Courage to tackle the things you can change.

3. A wise man: Knowing the difference between what you can and cannot change.

Part 1 – Just accept it: Accepting the things about your partner you cannot change

For our purposes, resisting the temptation to change our partner into what we believe to be the *ideal version* of her is part of accepting the things we cannot change. It also includes adopting the Win by Losing method and making a choice not to argue about matters unrelated to enforcing our ground rules. In doing so we are accepting the things we cannot change.

If, for example, our partner wants to buy brightly patterned furniture, then—unless this is related to one of our ground rules—we simply accept this is something we cannot change. At first, this may seem like losing but, by preserving our Emotional Energy for enforcement of our ground rules, the effect of accepting the things we cannot change means that we are able to take decisive action when needed; that is, when a ground rule needs to be enforced.

Exercise

Take a piece of paper and draw a line down the middle. On the left-hand side make a list of all the characteristics of your partner's personality (including her attitudes, values, beliefs, habits, and temperament), which you enjoy and would not want to change. These are the characteristics which, for most men, keep the two of you together. On the right-hand side, make a list of the characteristics which you would like to change if you were given the opportunity.

Where the characteristics on the left-hand side are concerned, you can be comforted and reassured to know that you won't wake up some day in the future to find your partner has changed, with all those positive attributes having suddenly disappeared. Equally, over time, her personality will probably remain unchanged and therefore she is unlikely to change fundamentally as the years go by. Those positive attributes which you like so much are happily here to stay.

Just as the personality characteristics on the left-hand side of the page are unlikely to change, you need to accept those characteristics listed on the right-hand side of the page will also remain unchanged. They are just as much part of your partner's personality as those items you wrote down on the left-hand side.

Generally speaking, people don't change and you can't make them change.

Don't waste your Emotional Energy trying to force your partner into changing a specific part of her personality. Just as the positive characteristics are there to stay, you are unlikely to succeed in your efforts to change what you see as her negative attributes.

Like you, your partner is only human. Deciding to accept your partner as she is, warts and all, can only be your decision. This, of course, isn't a one-way street and your partner needs to make the same decision about you. Remember to tear up the piece of paper which lists your partner's positive and negative attributes into small pieces before disposing of it!

Looking for the perfect person? Looked in the mirror recently? Your partner is perfectly imperfect – just like you – just like all of us.

We have established the inability of your partner to change for you. We have also discussed ground rules in Chapters 2 and 4. You may ask if enforcing your ground rules could be used as a way of changing your partner. The answer is absolutely not. There is a fundamental difference between asking your partner to respect your ground rules and trying to change an aspect of her personality.

A harsh reality: When ground rules collide

We have assumed that most people are fair, reasonable and want to get on well together. However, if your ground rules are fundamentally incompatible with your partner's, if she simply cannot live with them, or you are unable to live with hers, then this becomes a question of compatibility. You need to ask if the two of you are compatible and therefore if you are with the right person for you. By applying the type of approach detailed throughout this book most people, but not all, are able to adjust their communication and find ways of living happily with each other's ground rules.

Most people enjoy a low level of water in the Sink of Negativity and the associated happiness it brings – most people; but not everyone.

Part 2 – Facing up to your reality: Courage to tackle the things you can change

Where relationships and change are concerned, it's not your partner you can change, but your communication with her. Adopting just a few of the ideas contained in this book will change your communication and therefore the way in which you interact together. This, in turn, will lead to a change in the way you behave together. Change, therefore, can only come from you.

Change your communication to change the way you interact and behave together.

Adopting the Winning by Losing method and those principles outlined within each of the five Relationship Enablers may mean communicating in a different way with your partner from now on. This may not be easy at first and takes courage, if you have not communicated in this way before. If you have not yet started to apply our approach, we recommend reading Chapter 9 – I Am Safe: Comfort Zones.

A constructive approach: How to tackle a major area of concern

Do you have a major area of concern in your relationship? Perhaps your partner's friendship with a former boyfriend is irritating or worrying you. Perhaps it seems your partner's friends are more important to her than your relationship, or your partner has children from a previous relationship which are causing friction between you.

It can be difficult to tackle an area of concern with your partner. It's not unusual for the one topic of conversation, which is the most difficult to raise and discuss in a calm and constructive way, to also be the most important. Arguments related either directly or indirectly to the area of concern only serve to increase the amount of negativity in the Sink of Negativity. They rarely, if ever, resolve the issue.

Creating the right context before having this type of conversation is key to achieving a successful outcome. This means you spend some time actively:

- Adopting the Win by Losing method;
- Communicating and enforcing your ground rules clearly;
- Respecting your partner's ground rules;
- Listening with intent *every single day*;
- Spending quality time together;
- Showing affection (not to be confused with intimacy) every day;
- Making ten positive remarks for every negative remark;
- Accepting those things about your partner which you cannot change.

By adopting this approach, over a period of time (which is different for each relationship) you will create a positive context whereby you can have an open and honest conversation about your area of concern. What the

Win by Losing method does, in conjunction with communicating in a way which is consistent with the five Relationship Enablers, is to steadily empty the Sink of Negativity. This, in turn, opens the channels of communication between you and your partner, thus creating the context for a constructive conversation about your area of concern. Unless they are connected, if you have more than one area of concern, tackle one at a time. Don't tackle the second one until the first has been fully resolved.

When you feel the context and time is right, you should sit down with your partner and explain you have a major area of concern with your relationship. With open channels of communication and a positive context created by having an almost empty Sink of Negativity —the concern itself will prevent your sink being completely empty—you may be pleasantly surprised to hear what your partner has to say.

Stay calm throughout the conversation, but stick to the point. You shouldn't need to rely on your Emotional Energy when having this type of conversation; it's not an argument but a constructive conversation about resolving a specific aspect of your relationship which is an area of concern for you.

When tackling an area of concern, it's helpful to focus on what you want rather than what you don't want. This means you should focus on moving toward your preferred resolution rather than blaming your partner for something she has, or hasn't, done or said in the past. It doesn't matter how long ago the area of concern was formed, and pointing fingers is pointless. If you can't forgive and let go of the negative emotion you are not going to get the result you want.

Don't look back, look positively to the future.

To forgive is the highest, most beautiful form of love. In return, you will receive untold peace and happiness.

ROBERT MULLER, FORMER ASSISTANT
SECRETARY GENERAL, UNITED NATIONS

When tackling an area of concern, there may be setbacks at first, but persevere and have patience as it will take time for the changes to take place. If the area of concern has been in place over a relatively long period of time, it's reasonable to expect the solution may take several months to settle down.

In addition to courage, patience and persistence are certainly needed when making these types of important and potentially fundamental changes to your relationship.

Part 3 – A wise man: Knowing the difference between what you can and cannot change

There is a clear difference between accepting your partner as she is (and not trying to change her), and having the courage to adopt the suggestions and techniques contained in this book. This is because we are concerned with changing the way *you* communicate with your partner, rather than trying to change your partner's personality in some way.

We hope that we have made a clear distinction between the two and that this book contains the wisdom needed to put all this into practice. In any event, what you will need is courage and determination; something we can't give you from the pages of a book. You also need to understand comfort zones (see Chapter 9).

Make that change: Taking action

There are two types of people who will read this book: The first will read the book, think about the ideas it contains, and wonder why nothing in their lives has changed; the second will read this book and make an active effort to put into practice those ideas which they feel will work best for them. These are the ones who will notice a positive long-term improvement in their relationships and their lives. Which type are you?

Key Points

1. Accept the things you know that you cannot change in your partner and therefore in your relationship.

2. Change comes from within you by communicating in a different and better way with your partner. Win by Losing. The choice is yours.

3. The Win by Losing method and five Relationship Enablers have the potential to transform the way you communicate together. It creates the context for you to address an area of concern in a constructive and effective manner by lowering the Sink of Negativity and therefore improving the way you communicate.

4. It's important to have the wisdom or self-awareness—some people call this "emotional intelligence"—to know the difference between what you can and cannot change in your relationship.

Questions and Answers

Q: Why have you included a prayer in your book?

A: No matter what you believe in (or not), this particular prayer is about being able to distinguish the things we can and cannot change, having the courage to change the things we can, and the wisdom to know the difference. That's important in our relationship and, for that matter, in life in general.

Q: Does not being able to change my partner mean the way we communicate will also never change?

A: No. In most cases, communicating in a different way is entirely possible when you adopt the Win by Losing method and communicate in a way which is consistent with the five Relationship Enablers.

Q: I have a major area of concern with my relationship, but either I never find the right time to raise it as an issue, or whenever I try to talk about it we end up arguing. What can I do?

A: It's possible to resolve any major area of concern within a context of an almost empty Sink of Negativity and open channels of communication between you and your partner. This can be achieved by following the Win by Losing method and the points listed earlier in this chapter. When you have created a constructive context, you will be able to have the type of conversation needed to achieve the outcome you seek. Depending on what the issue is and how much negative energy is currently in your, your partner's, and your relationship's Sinks of Negativity (see Chapter 2 for more details), it may take some time to create the appropriate positive context.

Q: I have got this far in your book and thought about some changes to the way I communicate with my partner, but my relationship hasn't changed yet. Is that normal?

A: Thinking about communicating in a better way with your partner is certainly the first step, but for change to take place, you need to TAKE ACTION.

Multiple Choice

1. The Serenity Prayer by Reinhold Niebuhr has been included in this book because:

    a. Reinhold Niebuhr's family is giving us a 5 percent commission on all merchandise they sell.

    b. If we pray hard enough, our partners will change for us. They won't change that part of their personality we like; they'll change the part we don't like into exactly what we were hoping for. It's easy for people to change.

    c. It's a break from the potentially time-consuming business of communicating in a constructive way with our partners.

    d. It provides us with valuable insight into distinguishing between what we can and can't change in our relationship.

2. The best way to get the most from this book is to:

   a. Keep a copy under your pillow.

   b. Give your partner a copy and explain the book is written by men for men, so she should take this into account when reading it.

   c. Read it all the way through from the beginning to the end and take action.

   d. Give a copy of the book to your partner's mother and ask her to summarize its content to her daughter.

3. We are all human and that means:

   a. We are always right and never make mistakes.

   b. Sometimes we get things wrong. Depending on the circumstances it might be appropriate to apologize for our actions.

   c. We don't have to take responsibility for our actions. No matter what happens, it's always someone else's fault.

   d. Our partners are perfect too. They never make mistakes either and they also don't need to take responsibility for their actions.

4. Your partner will change her personality for you because:

   a. That's what people do when they are in love. They only want to make their partner happy, and making changes to their personality for someone else is easy to do.

   b. Change comes from your partner and has nothing to do with you. It's her problem even though you're the one who wants her to change.

   c. It's been proven that people change because someone else wants them to change.

   d. None of the above.

5. The best way of handling a concern you have about your relationship is to:

    a. Think about it all of the time. Your partner's superhuman mind-reading powers will ensure she becomes aware of the issue and how to resolve it.

    b. Argue about it at every opportunity. If you argue about it often enough, you're guaranteed to find a solution. It doesn't matter how these arguments affect the Sink of Negativity.

    c. Adopt the Win by Losing method and communicate in a way which is consistent with the five Relationship Enablers to create the right context with an almost empty Sink of Negativity, for a constructive and open conversation about how to find a long-term resolution to the issue.

    d. Take your partner to expensive restaurants and buy her equally expensive presents in the hope the area of concern will somehow resolve itself.

Take Action

Take some time to answer and act upon these questions.

1. Do you have a "personality changes wish list" where your partner is concerned?

    •   Are these changes central to your happiness in your relationship? If yes, why are you in a relationship with her?

    •   If not, it's time to let that wish list go! Stop wasting your Emotional Energy trying to change her. It won't work.

2. Change can only come from within you.

    •   Have you accepted your partner can't change for you?

    •   If so, what impact did this have on your relationship?

3. Nobody is perfect. Has your partner accepted she can't change you?

- How do you know?

4. Imagine for a moment that your partner could indeed change for you. This being the case, everyone would be able to change for the people they love.

    - Think of a former girlfriend: If you had changed for her, what sort of person would you be today?

    - Don't ask what your partner can do for you, but what you might be able to do for her.

5. Do you have an area of concern which you would like to discuss with your partner?

    - Creating the right context is key to achieving a successful outcome. This is something only you can do.

    - You can create the context needed to resolve an area of concern when you have:

        1. Adopted the Win by Losing method;

        2. Communicated and enforced your ground rules clearly;

        3. Respected your partner's ground rules;

        4. Listened with Intent *every single day*;

        5. Spent quality time together;

        6. Shown affection (not to be confused with intimacy) every day;

        7. Made ten positive remarks for every negative remark; and

        8. Accepted those things about your partner which you cannot change.

    - Only then will you be well placed to have a constructive conversation about any concern you may have about your relationship. These eight points will create the positive and open context needed to have this type of conversation and enable you to achieve the outcome you seek.

- Does your partner have areas of concern too? How do you know? Have you asked and encouraged her to talk about them (preferably one at a time)?

What's Next?

In the next chapter we will introduce you to the 5th Relationship Enabler – Say what you mean: Straight Talking, which is all about being direct.

CHAPTER 8

Say what you mean: Straight Talking

The single biggest problem in communication is the illusion that it has taken place.

GEORGE BERNARD SHAW

Why read this chapter? What's in it for you?

In this chapter we will cover:

► Say what you mean and mean what you say: What Straight Talking is about and why it matters;

► Nobody is a mind reader: Say what needs to be said;

► Compromise: It really can work;

► Not like you: Understanding the way your partner thinks;

► Thinking about nothing: An easy way to handle this issue;

► Three simple games: Ways to spot and deal with them;

► The trickiest topic of all: How to increase levels of intimacy;

► Giving high levels of intimacy a chance: How to deal with modern technology;

► Key Points;

► Questions and Answers;

- ▶ Multiple Choice;

- ▶ Take Action;

- ▶ What's Next?

Let's make a start: Introduction

Say what you mean: Straight Talking is our 5th Relationship Enabler.

What we say is not always what we mean. Even when we say exactly what we mean and it makes sense to us, our partners may not understand what it is we are trying to say. When in a relationship we tend to assume our loved ones understand what we mean. We communicate in a way which is clear to us—we understand what *we* mean when *we* say it.

The same cannot be said about our partners, who are on the receiving end of our communication. This ambiguity doesn't always matter, but at other times it's important and can lead to unnecessary friction and upset.

Adopting the right approach: Assertive vs. aggressive communication

There are no prizes for appreciating the fact that women respond far more positively to assertive as opposed to aggressive communication. Only stupid men think being aggressive will, in the long term, get them what they want where women are concerned.

Being assertive means saying what you need to say in a clear and thought-out way, while ensuring you do not become angry, or degrade the person with whom you are communicating.

Your partner may not want to hear some home truths, but under these circumstances and in this context that doesn't matter. Communicating in an assertive manner means you don't need to hold in anything that you need to get off your chest. If there is something which you need to say, then say it to the person who can do something about it. In this case, that's your partner.

Only stupid men think being aggressive with women will get them what they want.

Let's be clear about this: If there is something on your mind, something which you just can't leave in the past then you must say it. Equally, you are far more likely to achieve your preferred outcome when you have taken the time and put in the effort needed to create a positive context with a virtually empty Sink of Negativity and open channels of communication as covered in Chapter 7.

Before the conversation, think carefully what you will say and how you will say it. In most cases, the more time you spend preparing what you want to say, the more likely your communication will be clear, concise, and nonaggressive. Making sure you are feeling calm at the start of the conversation is also vital. If you are angry before you even start, you will come across as aggressive rather than assertive.

Think before you speak, be calm, so your message is absorbed.

If someone you know disagrees with you in an aggressive way, do you stop and think, "You know, even though they're being aggressive toward me, I really understand their point"? No, of course not. All you hear is the aggression; the words no longer matter. Women are the same as men in this respect. If you want to get your point across effectively, you need to be assertive, not aggressive.

If you are aggressive or rude, your partner will tune out and stop listening. Sometimes aggressive people say things that, if said respectfully and calmly, are actually rational and sensible. Don't let your delivery ruin your message!

If something needs to be said, then you must say it in a calm and respectful manner. Win by Losing. The choice is yours.

What am I thinking about? Nobody is a mind reader

Straight Talking is also concerned with saying *what you need to say* to the person *who needs to hear* it most, in an open and honest way. While it is easier to complain to someone else about your partner, the only person who can help you solve it is your partner. Man up, be respectful and calm and talk to her!

Women are not mind readers!

You can talk about anything with your partner as long as you plan what you are going to say and approach the conversation in a calm and respectful way. This is certainly true when your Sink of Negativity is nearly empty and you are communicating well. You'll be surprised how well your partner responds.

Don't tell the world about your issue, tell your partner. The world can't help.

Finding agreement: Compromise

According to Merriam-Webster, to compromise is defined as, "come to agreement by mutual concession," or "find or follow a way between extremes." Both sides give up something in order to find agreement on a specific issue.

International diplomacy is full of examples where no one gets everything they want, but an agreement is reached which meets the needs of both parties.

Of course, there are times in a relationship where compromise does take place. If one of you wants a beach holiday and the other prefers exploring new places, there are plenty of holidays which accommodate both. Half the time can be spent relaxing in the sun and the other half exploring. That said, there are plenty of times where compromise doesn't work in this way. As long as it doesn't affect your ground rules then it's unlikely to matter. This means that unless the compromise puts pressure on your ground rules, there is little to gain by arguing your point. Don't have an argument that you are likely to lose about unimportant things, save your Emotional Energy for defending your ground rules.

Generally speaking, compromises in relationships exist because they work for women. It's an effective way of persuading men to do what they want them to do in a constructive context. This reduces or completely removes the friction commonly associated with men not getting what they want. From a Win by Losing perspective, this doesn't matter.

It may surprise you: Understanding your partner

To communicate in a way which is consistent with the Straight Talking Relationship Enabler, you need to appreciate how your partner thinks. This section will provide you with an insight into the considerable differences between the way men and women think, especially where emotions are concerned.

In this section, it is necessary for us to develop an understanding of "metacognition." American developmental psychologist John H. Flavell defined metacognition in 1979 as: "Thinking about your own thinking."

The root "meta" means "beyond," so the term refers to "beyond thinking." Specifically, this means that it includes the processes of planning, tracking, and assessing your own understanding or performance.

As human beings, we are aware of our own existence. We have an awareness of how we feel. If we feel happy, we are aware of the fact that we feel happy. If we feel angry, we are aware of feeling angry. An awareness of how we feel at any one time affects our thoughts, the way we communicate, and what we say.

We all have the ability to be aware of how we feel, but although we can't be definite, it's likely a Guinea Pig, for example, doesn't have this ability. They don't have the psychological capacity to be aware of the fact they feel threatened; they just have the feeling of being threatened until the threat passes.

No matter how we feel—happy, sad, reflective, regretful, jealous—we are always aware of the fact that we feel that way.

In addition, we are also able to think about and consider what it means to feel that way. Generally, men are able to hold one or two *levels* of emotion in their mind at any one time. They could, for example, feel anger and, because of feeling angry and being aware of it, also feel regret.

Women, on the other hand, hold a great many levels in their minds at the same time. In fact, women are incredibly good at this and are experts compared to men. For example, let's say Jane and Peter break up after five years of being together. How do we expect they feel about this? Perhaps Peter will be upset but, as time passes, he might also be annoyed with himself for being upset for so long. He will experience both emotions at the same time because he is aware of experiencing the first one.

In other words, if he had not been aware of the fact that he was upset, he would not have started to be annoyed with himself about feeling upset. That's metacognition in action. Peter only feels annoyed with himself because he's aware that he feels upset. Peter will probably be able to hold the feeling of upset and annoyance in his mind at the same time.

As with most women, Jane's feelings are completely different in this situation. First, she may feel upset, then angry about feeling upset. Then she feels regret that she was angry. Then she starts to question herself about feeling regretful, as she has decided there is nothing to feel regretful about. She is strong and she won't let her feelings of regret be caused by Peter. Then she feels annoyed with Peter for causing her to feel regret, and so on.

The important point is that Jane, like most women, is able to hold all these emotions in her head *at the same time*. This means her emotional response to any situation can come from any of these emotional levels. From a man's perspective, it's impossible to know which one.

So, when communicating with your partner, she will have multiple levels of emotions in her mind at the same time. For instance, she could be upset about something you did or didn't do, and then be annoyed with the fact that she felt upset. This could trigger a memory of when she had been annoyed about being upset on another occasion with you. Then, because of that memory, she might feel regretful that this has happened twice!

When your partner communicates with you, that communication could be coming from any of these emotional levels. Sometimes your partner may say something, or act in a particular way, which makes no sense to you. She may bring up something which, to your mind, has nothing to do with what's being discussed at that moment. To your partner, with multiple emotional levels and complex connections between those levels, it all makes perfect sense. Never underestimate the differences between the way men and women think.

As the philosopher George Santayana once said, "When men and women agree, it is only in their conclusions; their reasons are always different."

It is extremely important to take metacognition into account as it goes some way to explaining why men don't always understand their partner's way of thinking, or their communication. This is because women can react to different "emotional levels," or a unique combination of emotional levels, which the typical man can't anticipate.

Women were built to be emotional multitaskers by design, given the biological imperative of handling a partner, children, and home all at the same time. Men should not try to second-guess why their partners behave in a particular way. Their reasoning, the thought processes which take place in their minds are fundamentally different from men—especially where intimate relationships are concerned.

A man skill: Thinking about nothing

A typical woman's ability to hold so many emotions in her mind concurrently is impressive. However, it also explains why women can't understand how men can think about nothing at all.

A woman finds it hard to believe a man when he achieves the seemingly impossible act—to a woman—of "thinking about nothing". This is because, with their complex multiple levels of thought, women are unable to think about nothing, and cannot comprehend the idea that this is possible. For a man, it's actually relatively easy.

In *The Tale of Two Brains*, marriage expert Mark Gungor explored the differences between the way men and women think. It's worth watching the section on what Mark terms "The Nothing Box"; that is, the typical man's way of thinking about nothing (see https://youtu.be/3XjUFYxSxDk). Your partner should watch it too as it explains, amongst other things, why men are able to think about nothing, in an insightful and entertaining way.

Most men have experienced that moment when they are relaxing and their partner asks, "What's on your mind? Penny for your thoughts."

The man answers, "Nothing, just relaxing."

The woman says "Why can't you share how you are feeling and share your thoughts? I tell you everything."

When your partner asks you what you are thinking, if you are actually thinking about nothing and your partner has watched *The Tale of Two Brains*, tell her you have opened your "nothing box".

Women don't have a "nothing box" so are unable to think about nothing at all.

The complexity of your partner's mind: The emotional spider's web

Generally speaking, if you can't say anything nice to your partner it's better not to say anything at all. Why? When your partner hears the words you say to her, they pass through an emotional spider's web and the hurtful or negative words become trapped.

If you only have *one* spider's web there are large gaps between the silk and the emotion attached to those words passes through the web quite easily. However, with two emotional levels in your head, there are two spiders' webs and the emotional words are more likely to become caught up in one of the two webs. Each emotional level has its own spider's web so, as you can imagine, women have considerably more of these emotional spiders' webs than men. Those negative words don't stand a chance of passing through and easily become entangled in one of the many webs.

Nothing good comes out of the words caught in these emotional webs. They cause us to think about the words all the time and overanalyze them. They cause further friction and arguments, and the water level in our Sink of Negativity to rise.

*Negative emotionally charged words **hurt** your partner for far longer than most men appreciate, are analyzed to the nth degree, and come back to haunt you when you least expect them—probably during an argument.*

You may have had the experience where one minute you are arguing with your partner about one thing and the next she refers to something you said to her three weeks earlier. You can't remember what you said to her three weeks ago, so you just deny it. The next moment the argument becomes about what you said three weeks ago.

By the time one or both of you run out of the Emotional Energy needed to keep arguing, you've forgotten what started the argument in the first place. Nothing is resolved, you are both annoyed with each other and your Sink of Negativity is left fuller than when you started.

You are also now annoyed that your partner threw in something which had nothing to do with the argument. So, not only did the current argument not achieve anything, but you now have something else to be annoyed with her about.

Women behaving in this way can be interpreted by men as *unreasonable* or *manipulative*. Others may see it as a curve ball. Well, guess what? *You* put those negative words out there and you are responsible for those words now being entangled in all those emotional webs of hers.

Your partner won't understand your angry reaction when you can't understand why she brought up points or previous arguments which, to you, were irrelevant to the matter at hand. However, to her, they are as fresh as the day you put those words there. Unless you were enforcing a ground rule, you placed words in her mind unnecessarily. It didn't need to be this way. Win by Losing. The choice is yours.

Talking time: Letting it all out

For women, talking about how they feel reduces the strength of the emotions associated with the words caught in their emotional webs. The more they talk, the better they feel. That's why, if you listen to a woman talking to her upset friend on the phone, most of the time you won't hear any advice at all, just "Really?" "How dreadful," "Oh dear," "What did he say?" "Goodness me," and so on.

The telephone conversation will continue in this way for quite a long time. She knows instinctively that her upset friend needs to get it all out. She's just listening as her friend is in, what a man would understand to be *offload mode*, while at the same time she's providing just enough feedback to ensure her friend knows everything being said is being taken in. When she is like this she is not asking for a solution, she just wants to be listened to. Many men make the mistake of trying to find a solution and that actually will aggravate their partner.

Can you imagine an upset man giving this level of detail to his friend? Instead, they'd go for a drink, the upset man would give a brief summary of what had happened, they would both agree life sucked, and then probably spend the rest of the evening talking about TV and football.

So, when your partner is upset about someone or something *which doesn't involve you* and she won't stop talking about it, now you know why.

When your partner is upset, just do your best to let her get it out of her system, and don't try to fix it, just listen.

Equally, when you are stressed or upset she will assume you want to talk because that works so well for her. Just tell her that you are not upset with her and she needs to give you some space. It's likely she won't believe you at first, but being firm and consistent means that she will get the message eventually.

Your negative words really stick: Flypaper

When you and your partner have an argument have you noticed how normally the anger passes for you more quickly than for your partner? You've had your say and, after a relatively short period of time, you don't feel annoyed any more. You've got it out your system and have calmed down.

Contrast that with your partner. She's more likely to stay annoyed for a long, long time. It's like having two different types of flypaper: yours isn't sticky, the anger has passed, and those flies which represent your anger have detached themselves and flown away; your partner's flypaper is completely different—she has incredibly sticky flypaper and negative emotions become well and truly stuck; those flies, which represent negative emotions, are going nowhere, and you're in trouble!

How do you transform her flypaper into something a lot less sticky? Often this is through the giving of a "peace gift," such as flowers and chocolates. It's not surprising that virtually all peace gifts are from men to women. Most women have far stickier flypaper than men and this one inescapable fact supports a large part of global floristry.

There's nothing wrong with having an argument. There's nothing wrong with losing your temper once in a while. We're all human. Just be aware that when you have had your say and the anger has passed, you need to recognize that the anger hasn't passed for your partner, which puts you at a real disadvantage.

Her strong, lingering, negative emotions will drive the way she communicates with you for much longer than is the case for you.

Under these circumstances, depending upon what the argument was about, some women respond well to being given flowers. This will have the effect of releasing those remaining strong negative emotions from her flypaper. For other women, of course, this will make no difference at all.

Playtime: Communication games

In his book *Games People Play*, Eric Berne examined the idea of people playing games as part of their day-to-day communication, normally without even realizing that's what they were doing. In this section we are going to cover three simple games which you need to avoid, if you are to truly Win by Losing.

Game 1: What if...?

The first game is called "What if…?" Women and men in equal measure play this game extremely well. This is an example of how it works:

"I really don't know what to do. What do you think?"

"Hmm. I see what you mean. Have you tried calling her?"

"*What if* she doesn't want to talk to me?"

"How about sending her a text first?"

"*What if* she ignores it?"

"Have you spoken to Jane about this? She could help."

"*What if* Jane is also annoyed about it?"

No matter what suggestions are made, the reply normally contains "What if…?" at the beginning of the sentence. It's a way of the other person avoiding the issue and finding excuses, no matter what you say to them. If you recognize this game, you need to call it out by saying something like,

"You're playing 'What if…?' with me. I've given you all the suggestions I can think of. The next step is up to you."

The alternative is to be sucked into the "What if…?" game. That's not going to help your partner resolve the issue and will probably become a source of annoyance for you.

Game 2: Yes, but...

The second of our games is called "Yes, but…," which can be extremely annoying for the person on the receiving end. It's similar to "What if…?" so we will use the same example,

"I really don't know what to do."

"I see what you mean. Have you tried calling her?"

"*Yes, but* she won't want to talk to me."

"How about sending her a text first?"

"*Yes, but* she'll ignore it."

"Have you spoken to Jane about this? She could help."

"*Yes, but* Jane is also annoyed about it."

Treat the "Yes, but..." game in the same way as "What if...?" You can only provide suggestions. The next step isn't up to you—it's up to your partner. This is *their* issue, not yours, and playing "Yes, but..." with you isn't going to help them solve it.

Game 3: Hooked

Finally, you need to be aware of your *hooks* as we can guarantee your partner knows them extremely well. Don't get *hooked*, as it won't end well for you. An example of getting *hooked* is as follows:

"Well, that evening with Andrew and Sue was a disaster."

"I don't want to talk about it. I'm going to bed."

"I can't believe they behaved that way and you agreed with them! It was embarrassing."

"Well, that's the way it turned out. I'm going to bed. It's late and I've got work tomorrow."

"Typical man! Sue's just like your mother."

"No, she's not. How can you say that? If you actually took an interest in my mother, you might get to know her."

Our guy here didn't want to argue with his partner. He only wanted to get some sleep, and almost managed it, until he grabbed the hook his partner dangled in front of him—the comment about his mother. It was at that point that he could no longer ignore what his partner was saying. He felt the need to react. Once he had reacted and had played into the "hook" game, the unnecessary argument had started.

His partner almost certainly didn't make a conscious decision to use a *hook*. That's not how these things work. Nevertheless, it's an effective way of pulling someone into an argument.

Let's also be clear about *hooks*. Men use them just as easily and regularly as women. Hooks are a normal part of the way we all communicate. However, being aware of hooks, and which specific hooks reel you in, can be quite liberating. Once identified, they lose their emotional power and control.

What's your hook? What could your partner say to you that would reel you in just like a fish on a fishing line? The next time you encounter a *hook*, just smile to yourself, call it out for what it really is "That's a hook and I don't want to play," and let it go. Don't waste your Emotional Energy by getting hooked.

The trickiest topic of all: Improving levels of intimacy

There are times in every relationship when levels of intimacy are lower than we would like. Depending on the reason for this, we may find matters correct themselves relatively quickly. However, when this isn't the case it has a much more damaging and destructive effect on the relationship than most women appreciate.

If levels of intimacy are too low in your relationship, it doesn't have to be this way. There is action you can take to improve matters. This process isn't easy; it will take time, effort, and patience. There's no quick fix.

That said the first step is to remove all the other major areas of concern (see Chapter 7 for more details) before tackling this tricky topic. We're not just talking about your areas of concern; your partner many have areas of concern too and they also need to be resolved.

There's little point trying to improve levels of intimacy if there are other areas of concern on your or your partner's mind which are causing friction between you. In fact, low levels of intimacy are often a consequence of too much negativity in one or all of the Sinks of Negativity (see Chapter 2), and the resulting emotional barriers between you. Take action to create the context where these are resolved and all three Sinks of Negativity are either empty or almost empty. Then you may find levels of intimacy improve over time without you having to address the issue directly.

Resolving areas of concern and having empty Sinks of Negativity is the most effective starting point where improving levels of intimacy is concerned.

Throughout this book we have avoided the buying of gifts as a way to somehow improve your relationship. Being able to communicate in a way which is consistent with the five Relationship Enablers does not have anything to do with your personal wealth. In any event, buying expensive gifts, going out to lavish restaurants or on expensive holidays together will only bring short-term relief. What we are interested in here is a long-term solution to getting what you want from your relationship.

So how do you increase levels of intimacy in a way which doesn't have to cost you anything and is sustainable in the long term? You can achieve this by creating the **right context** for your relationship to change in a way which promotes and supports higher levels of intimacy.

This is achieved by communicating in a way where you adopt the Win by Losing method and apply each of the five Relationship Enablers in every situation with your partner, to the fullest extent. Specifically, to increase levels of intimacy, you need to create a context where you have virtually empty Sinks of Negativity and well-developed channels of communication between you and your partner. This is the same list as with creating the context needed to resolve any area of concern being:

- Adopting the Win by Losing method;
- Communicating and enforcing your ground rules clearly;
- Respecting your partner's ground rules;

- Listening with intent *every single day*;

- Spending quality time together;

- Showing affection (not to be confused with intimacy) every day;

- Making ten positive remarks for every negative remark;

- Accepting those things about your partner which you cannot change.

The most important difference to resolving an area of concern and improving levels of intimacy is the need to *resolve all your and your partner's other areas of concern* before tackling this issue. You need to create the right context before levels of intimacy can improve. As we explained in Chapter 1, context is everything.

Levels of intimacy in any relationship can be improved, but it takes time and perseverance. Don't kid yourself that an easy option is to find someone else. The same patterns will build up over time with a different partner, and you will eventually find yourself back at square one where levels of intimacy are concerned. Rather than spend all that time, energy, and probably money on finding someone else, why not use the techniques and methods described in this book to improve levels of intimacy with your current partner?

Whether or not you choose to make these changes is, of course, entirely up to you. This isn't going to be easy and it could be a bumpy and at times unpredictable ride. It depends how important increasing levels of intimacy are to you. Win by Losing. The choice is yours.

She's not like you: Everything matters

Although it's possible to tackle low levels of intimacy *in the appropriate context of applying the Win by Losing method and each of the points listed above*, it's also important to keep in mind that the way men think about intimacy is completely different from how women think about it.

Although high levels of intimacy are equally enjoyable for women, context and meaning are far more important—from a woman's perspective their stars need to align.

The context and meaning must be right for women to be in the mood, which means that everything that happens between you matters...a lot.

Yes, that's right *everything*. Your partner remembers it all: every disagreement, every argument, every time you were too busy watching TV to listen or help her out, every time you let her change the baby's dirty diaper (if you have children), every time you were too busy to help out her friends or parents, every time you made a critical or nasty remark.

Equally, she will also remember every time you said something nice or complimentary, every time you helped out at home (assuming you live together), every time you Won by Losing, every time you had a calm and constructive conversation, every time you were affectionate to her, every time you listened with intent. Your partner will remember all that too. Keep that in mind the next time you can't understand why she turns out the lights and goes to sleep.

Everything matters: Women remember it all.

There's something in the air tonight: Aligning her stars

In order to understand why someone—anyone—communicates or behaves in a particular way, we need to ask ourselves what we would do, how we would behave in their position: for example, a soldier in war who carries his fallen comrade from the war zone; an unfortunate householder who defends their property from a burglar by killing the intruder; a once-successful businessman now serving time in prison for tax evasion, and so on.

How would we have behaved if we had faced the same challenges, the same situation or life choices? If their actions make some sort of sense to us, in terms of how we would have behaved if the same had happened to us, we can understand them better.

We undertake the same type of analysis and interpretation with our partners. If your partner isn't interested in high levels of intimacy, you may think to yourself, "She doesn't want to have an intimate relationship with me because she's being manipulative."

However, you are coming to that conclusion because as a man, if *you* behaved in the same way, it would be because *you* were being manipulative with her. When we adopt this way of thinking we assume women think the same way as men. This assumption is fundamentally flawed and leads to incorrect interpretations of why women act in the way that they do. Sure, if a man were to behave in this way it would probably be because he was trying to be manipulative. That's not normally the case where women are concerned.

As we said earlier in this chapter, women connect recent events and intimacy. It's important to understand this—it's not because they are trying to be manipulative, but because the wider context for women is far more important than for men. That context includes how they feel about the relationship and what has happened recently between the two of you.

Men are able to separate recent events and intimacy. Women, on the other hand, connect the two.

*Intimacy for women is a consequence of the relationship **working for them**, not a consequence of wanting to be intimate.*

By adopting the Win by Losing method, and communicating in a way which is consistent with the five Relationship Enablers, you will be able to create the context where there are no issues with the relationship (from your partner's perspective), and *her stars really do align*. With this context in place, any conversation with your partner to tackle low levels of intimacy is far more likely to yield a positive outcome for you.

It's often said that for every negative remark or comment, there should be ten positive remarks. This helps to keep the Sink of Negativity virtually empty. Most men expect high levels of intimacy irrespective of what else has happened between them and their partner recently, and just expect their partner's stars to be aligned.

Saying positive things to each other must certainly be a universal joint ground rule. Do this every day.

Start counting: Twinkle, twinkle

In the previous section, as we have mentioned, women need to have all their stars aligned in order for you to experience high levels of intimacy together. Recall in Chapter 2, we introduced the idea that initially, relationships exist in a vacuum, but over time they become more complex due to internal factors, such as our own expectations of the relationship (which are often a consequence of social, religious and economic norms), and external factors, such as friends, family, work, money, and running a home.

Eventually, more pressures start to impact on the relationship. As far as high levels of intimacy are concerned, each one is a star. At first, it's easy to align those stars because there only a few in the sky. Over time, more stars appear and alignment can potentially become more difficult. How do you align those stars, no matter how many there are? Create the right context by adopting the Win by Losing method and communicating in a way which is consistent with the five Relationship Enablers.

It doesn't matter how many stars your partner has in her sky; with time and effort, you can align them all.

Giving high levels of intimacy a chance: How to deal with modern technology

If you *want* to reduce levels of intimacy between you and your partner, or *fail to develop a new and positive way of communicating*, the quickest and easiest way of doing so is to spend as much time as you can on your smartphone.

Ignoring each other for hours on end in favor of that little screen helps too. Even better, take your smartphone into your bedroom and spend as much time staring at the screen as you can. Women really like it when you spend more time, and devote more attention to your smartphone, than to them. If you're lucky, you partner will be just as addicted to her smartphone as you probably are, so she won't notice the precious hour or so before you go to sleep being wasted away.

Don't worry about this though as everyone's doing it. That makes it right, doesn't it?

Does the number 29,200 mean anything to you?

How about 700,800?

These are important numbers. If you live to 80 years of age, 29,200 represents the number of days you have on this planet before your life comes to an end. If we multiply this number by 24, we find that living to 80 years gives us 700,800 hours of life. It's not much and what you do with those hours is up to you.

When you are very old and approaching your end, you will look back at the countless hours you have spent on your smartphone and consider all the other things you could have been doing instead: all the special experiences you missed, and the passion, closeness and love you wasted away by staring at that little screen.

As your life comes to an end, you will have the satisfaction of knowing how many hours of your short time on this planet were wasted on meaningless apps, *likes*, and social media friends, who never actually touched your life in a meaningful way. We should rejoice in the fact that so many apps were designed to be as addictive as humanly possible. Your life wouldn't have been the same without them—it wouldn't have been the same at all.

Using your smartphone before you go to bed can interfere with your sleeping patterns as the backlight delays the release of melatonin; a hormone important for a good night's sleep. That's perfect as, with a bit of luck, you will both be so constantly exhausted that passion will be the furthest thing from your minds.

If you really want to transform your love life, leave both smartphones in the kitchen when you go to bed.

We wonder if you can.

Key Points

1. Say what you mean and mean what you say. Just as you can't read your partner's mind, she can't read yours. Think it? Feel it? Then say it.

2. Most women hold multiple levels of thought and emotion in their mind at the same time. Your partner's emotional response can come from any of these emotional levels and it's rarely possible to know which one. Don't assume your partner thinks in the same way as you. She doesn't.

3. Where levels of intimacy are low in your relationship, apply the Win by Losing method and communicate in a way which is

consistent with the five Relationship Enablers to tackle this issue in a constructive way. Change the way you communicate to empty those Sinks of Negativity thereby creating strong channels of communication between you and your partner. Utilize the action points listed in this chapter to create a context where levels of intimacy improve.

4. It takes time, effort, and understanding to align those stars. Don't expect everything to *just work itself out*. Nobody said being in a happy intimate relationship was easy. It takes focus, time, patience, and effort. Win by Losing. The choice is yours.

Questions and Answers

Q: I'm upset about something that happened last week, but my partner still hasn't worked out what. What's going on?

A: Your partner is not a mind-reader. You must talk to her about it in a calm, constructive manner.

Q: When my partner asks me a question, does she always want an answer?

A: Not necessarily. She may just want you to listen to her. You need to be aware of this and check with her, rather than making that assumption.

Q: How can women hold multiple logical levels of thought and emotion in their heads at the same time? If men thought in the same way, it wouldn't be possible for them to function.

A: This can probably be explained in terms of complex biological differences between the way men and women's brains work, but that's outside the scope of this book.

Q: My partner is really annoyed with something I said the other day. Surely if it's her emotions, that's her issue, right?

A: You can keep telling yourself that if you like. The chances are that you put those words out there and that's why they have become entangled in one of her many emotional spiders' webs (there's one emotional spider's web for each level). Although we appreciate sometimes there aren't any other options, you might want to think twice about not putting words like that out again: unless, of course, you are enforcing one of your ground rules.

Q: What are "games" in the context of this book?

A: They are unconscious ways of communicating which you need to understand and handle in a positive way. We play many games and "What if…?" "Yes, but…," and "Hooked" are three examples.

Q: Are you suggesting I can improve levels of intimacy simply by applying the ideas contained in this book?

A: Yes, although you may find it takes time and effort to apply those ideas in a way which will achieve your desired outcome. Nothing of value comes easily in life and this is no exception.

Q: Why is it so much easier to enjoy high levels of intimacy when the relationship is new, compared to when we have been together for a long time?

A: For a woman to experience high levels of intimacy, her stars need to be aligned. The more internal and external forces exert pressure on the relationship, the more stars in her sky. Applying the Win by Losing method and communicating in a way which is consistent with the five Relationship Enablers every day will steadily align those stars.

Q: I really like using my mobile phone for about an hour before I go to sleep. My partner likes using her mobile phone too. This means we get changed for bed, use our mobile phones, and then go do sleep. Does this matter?

A: It's your life and your relationship. Win by Losing. The choice is yours.

Multiple Choice

1. You're sitting at home, minding your own business, thinking about nothing in particular. Your partner comes up to you and asks what you're thinking about. The best response is:

   a. Say you're not thinking about anything.

   b. Play a game with her and make out you were thinking about your relationship and some concerns you had. She won't go into overdrive and want to know more.

   c. Don't answer the question and quickly change the subject.

   d. Tell her you have opened your nothing box.

2. Your partner holds multiple levels of thought and associated emotions in her mind at the same time. This means:

   a. You should break up with her and find someone else instead. Not many women think in this way.

   b. It's easy for you to understand what's going on in her mind at any one time. If she says or does something which doesn't make sense to you, you should interpret it in terms of what you would have done in the same situation.

   c. You need to keep this in mind when communicating with her. All women think in this way and your partner is no exception.

   d. You should give up and go home. It's just not possible to communicate in a constructive way where women are concerned.

3. You had an argument the other day and you've already moved on. Your partner, on the other hand, is still really annoyed. That's her issue, not yours, right?

a. Sure. You don't need to concern yourself about that. Her Sink of Negativity won't be affected and she'll soon forget about it.

b. You need to get annoyed with her about the fact that she still hasn't let it go. Having another argument is a good way to clear the air.

c. You might be over it, but she isn't. That makes it a problem for both of you. Listening with intent would be a good start. Was the argument about a ground rule? If not, why didn't you Win by Losing?

d. Of course it's her problem. You also find discussing these issues with her mother a great way of helping her to move on.

4. The spider's web is:

a. A way of explaining how the words you use stay in your partner's mind for far longer than you might expect.

b. Of no importance as it doesn't matter how many of your words remain charged with negative emotion in your partner's mind.

c. The basis for playing a game, to see how many words can be stored this way. It's fun to place as many negatively charged words in your partner's mind; the more the merrier.

d. This isn't a metaphor and there is a real spider's web in your partner's mind.

5. For every negative remark to your partner, ten positive remarks are needed because:

a. You are keeping score.

b. It takes a lot more positive energy to overcome a smaller amount of negative energy. For most people, negative thoughts are more likely to linger than positive ones.

Generally speaking, ten positive remarks are equivalent to one negative remark.

c. Actually, we're kidding. Ten negative remarks for every positive one is much more fun. We like adding negative energy to the Sink of Negativity.

d. Forget about affection, what's needed here is some good old-fashioned intimacy. It works for you so it will work for her too.

6. You can improve levels of intimacy in your relationship by:

a. Ensuring you argue every day.

b. Making high levels of intimacy a ground rule. That, after all, is what ground rules are for.

c. Buying expensive gifts for her.

d. Adopting the approach outlined in this chapter and working to create the context needed to have this type of conversation with your partner.

7. High levels of intimacy and constant use of smartphones go well together because:

a. You are friends and *like* each other all the time.

b. The light from smartphones helps you to have a really good night's sleep.

c. There's nothing wrong with using smartphones and social networking. It's only an issue when you could be using the time to be more intimate or affectionate with your partner instead.

d. The more online friends you have, and the more regularly you communicate with them, the more intimate your relationship becomes.

Take Action

Take some time to answer and act upon these questions.

1. Are levels of intimacy too low in your relationship? Before raising this tricky issue, take the time to create a positive and constructive context in your relationship by:

    1. Adopting the Win by Losing method;

    2. Communicating and enforcing your ground rules clearly;

    3. Respecting your partner's ground rules;

    4. Listening with intent *every single day*;

    5. Spending quality time together;

    6. Showing affection (not to be confused with intimacy) every day;

    7. Making ten positive remarks for every negative remark;

    8. Accepting those things about your partner which you cannot change.

    *   When the amount of negative energy in the Sinks of Negativity are low (meaning you rarely argue and enjoy each other's company), raise your concerns in a constructive and forward-looking way.

2. How many layers of thought are in your head right now?

    *   How does that contrast with your partner?

    *   What does this mean about how you communicate with her?

3. Does your partner communicate with you in unpredictable ways?

    *   Have you assumed your partner thinks the same way as you? She doesn't!

4. Have you fed your partner's spiders webs with negatively charged words recently?

- How did that work out for you? Did it matter?

- Were you enforcing a ground rule?

- How could you have handled things differently?

5. Thinking about nothing?

    - What's the best way of handling this if your partner asks you about it?

6. Write down all the stars in your partner's sky.

    - Are the stars aligned? If not, what action do you need to take?

7. Have you made ten positive remarks for every negative one?

    - No? Why not? It doesn't cost anything.

    - Are you coming up against your comfort zone (see Chapter 9)?

8. Have you put your smartphone away before going to bed?

    - If there is room for improvement where intimacy is concerned, this is a good place to start.

What's Next?

In the next chapter we will introduce you to I am Safe: Comfort Zones, where you will learn how to identify your comfort zones, consider expanding them and how that affects your thoughts and communications.

PART III
Take Action

CHAPTER 9

I am Safe: Comfort Zones

Sometimes we have to step out of our comfort zones. We have to break the rules. And we have to discover the sensuality of fear. We need to face it, challenge it, dance with it.

KYRA DAVIS, NOVELIST

Why read this chapter? What's in it for you?

In this chapter we will cover:

- ▶ What stops you from communicating in a better way: Understanding your comfort zone;

- ▶ The freedom to do more: What expanding your comfort zone means to you;

- ▶ Making it happen: How to expand your comfort zone;

- ▶ Key Points;

- ▶ Questions and Answers;

- ▶ Multiple Choice;

- ▶ Take Action;

- ▶ What's Next?

Let's make a start: Introduction

Changing the way we communicate in any context—not exclusively where intimate relationships are concerned—can be surprisingly difficult. As Henry Ford said, "If you always do what you have always done, you will always get what you always got."

We normally do what we have always done because we are comfortable and familiar with behaving and communicating in that way.

What we have always done feels familiar and is easy to do. It's something as natural as walking up a flight of stairs; we don't think about taking each step with hesitation and deliberation, we just do it. It's inside our *comfort zone*. Where a way of communicating is outside our comfort zone, we tend to avoid it as it often feels uncomfortable. This is either because we have not communicated in that way before, or we know the new way of communicating is wrong; it's contrary to our values and beliefs. Clearly this chapter does not apply to the latter scenarios!

Understanding your Comfort Zone

Figure 9.1 reveals a dotted line around the person, which represents his comfort zone. There are some activities and ways of communicating which are *within* his comfort zone. We can see he is comfortable with complaining about poor customer service, driving at night, going to work, shopping, and traveling abroad. Whenever he comes across any of these activities which are within his comfort zone, he feels comfortable about them as they are easy for him to do. Going shopping is not a stressful experience!

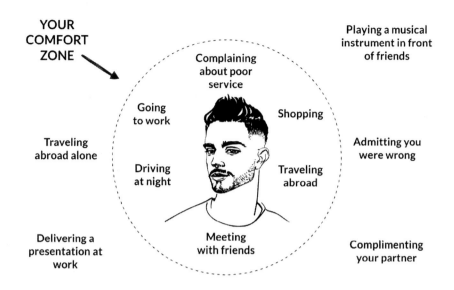

YOUR COMFORT ZONE

Playing a musical instrument in front of friends

Complaining about poor service

Going to work

Shopping

Traveling abroad alone

Admitting you were wrong

Driving at night

Traveling abroad

Delivering a presentation at work

Meeting with friends

Complimenting your partner

Figure 9.1. Comfort Zones in Action

However, there are also various examples of activities and forms of communication which are *outside* his comfort zone (Figure 9.1). Ask this person to deliver a presentation at work then his reaction will be far from relaxed. As the time approaches to deliver that presentation, for example, his heart rate will increase, he is likely to experience butterflies in his stomach, he will feel uncomfortable and experience all of this as *stress*. He will even try to find many reasons why he shouldn't pursue this course of action and deliver the presentation. These symptoms will become more intense as the time to deliver the presentation nears. Afterwards his heart rate will slow down again and all the other symptoms will disappear.

We can safely say that we have all experienced undertaking a task that was initially outside our comfort zone; it's an almost universal experience.

Stop for a moment and think of a time where you were asked to do something outside your comfort zone. As the time approached you would have become increasingly stressed about it. It's not a nice experience, and there's no doubt that it's a relief when it's all over. When the event outside your comfort zone has passed, your body returns to its normal self. The *outside comfort zone event* no longer presents a threat to you.

Size matters: Expanding your comfort zone

The experience of doing something *outside* your comfort zone has the effect of expanding it. The more you do the activity, which is initially outside your comfort zone, the more used to it you become, and you find that your comfort zone expands. Eventually, that activity which was stressful becomes familiar and comfortable; it's no longer a threat to you. This is when it's time to find new, more challenging activities to keep expanding your comfort zone.

Nobody looks back on their lives and wishes they had done less.

Notice we included "complimenting your partner" as something outside the person's comfort zone (Figure 9.1). This means he doesn't normally compliment her and any attempt to do so will lead to his body reacting in an adverse way by raising his heart rate, which encourages him not to go ahead with this approach.

We all have a comfort zone. We all have some activities within our comfort zones and other activities outside it. If you have been reading this book and have got this far without putting anything into practice, you need to start thinking about Win by Losing in terms of your comfort zone.

If you have considered talking to your partner about your ground rules, for example, but changed your mind at the last minute, that's your body reacting to communicating in a way which is *outside* your comfort zone. Notice how you suddenly felt far better when you decided *not* to talk about it—there's always another day.

If you let your comfort zone rule you, that day will never come. You will never find the right moment to put into practice the ideas contained in this book.

It's your comfort zone. It doesn't belong to anyone else.

You have a choice and you must have the determination to push through your body's natural reaction to communicating in a way which is initially outside your comfort zone. Win by Losing. The choice is yours.

Key Points

1. Everyone has a comfort zone. It's part of what makes us human. Changing the way we communicate in our relationship may mean communicating in a way which, at first, is outside our comfort zone. That's normal and to be expected.

2. Communicating in a different way with your partner may feel uncomfortable at first. That feeling is because you are doing something outside your comfort zone. However, by taking action, over a short period of time your comfort zone will expand and that uncomfortable feeling will disappear.

3. Completing the comfort zone exercise (see "Take action" below), or something similar, will demonstrate the feelings associated with communicating in a new and better way. It will also expand your comfort zone.

Questions and Answers

Q: Why does doing something new often feel uncomfortable?

A: If you haven't communicated in a certain way before, it can feel uncomfortable until you become used to it. That uncomfortable feeling is either because you know that you are doing something wrong, in which case you shouldn't be doing it at all, or the new action is outside your comfort zone.

Q: How long does it take for my comfort zone to expand and a new way of communicating to become natural and comfortable?

A: Not long at all. In a surprisingly short period of time, you will become use to it, and your comfort zone will have expanded.

Q: Do women also have comfort zones? Do they experience the same sort of feelings when they do something new or different?

A: Yes, comfort zones are not just for men!

Multiple Choice

1. If a new way of communicating is difficult or uncomfortable, you should:

   a. Give up. Nothing is worth that much effort.

   b. Appreciate that this will initially be outside your comfort zone and, with some determination and practice it will become natural and comfortable as your comfort zone expands.

   c. Talk to a professional psychotherapist about this, because it's not normal.

   d. Work out harder at the gym.

2. Completing the comfort zone exercise (see "Take Action" below), or something similar, will:

   a. Demonstrate to you how something uncomfortable will quickly become familiar as your comfort zone expands.

   b. Make no difference. If something new is hard or uncomfortable to do, it will always be that way.

   c. Only work if you take lots of multivitamins.

    d. Cause your comfort zone to shrink.

Take Action

Exercise

Unless the exercise we are about to describe is something you would *normally* do, it will help you to become better aware of the feelings and thoughts you experience as you near your comfort zone.

> *By completing this exercise, you will pass through your comfort zone thereby expanding it.*

The experience will also better prepare you for putting the ideas contained in this book into practice. This is especially the case if you decide to utilize our 90-day Action Plan (see Appendix 1), either instead of, or in conjunction with, acting upon the questions at the end of each chapter.

So, what's the exercise? All you need to do is to acknowledge the work of a service worker at least once a day for five consecutive days. You come across service workers every day: They serve you in restaurants, work in banks, call centers and offices; they keep the places you visit clean and tidy; they regularly make your lunch and clean up after you.

The next time you encounter a service worker, take an interest in them and thank them for the work they have done. Look at their name badge and use their name when thanking them. Of course, they are paid for their work, but that's not the point. You don't need to sit them down and have a fifteen-minute discussion. Just use their name and thank them for a job well done.

You may be surprised how well your good deed will be received. People tend to respond positively when we treat them with a little respect, and like fellow human beings. That's an obvious observation, but so many of us forget about it as we go about our often stressful, fast-paced, and hectic lives.

Be straight, be clear, show respect. Isn't that what you want from those around you?

Questions

Take some time to answer and act upon these questions.

1. Is communicating in a different way, as described in this book, *within* or *outside* your comfort zone?

    -   What does this mean about how you will feel when you change your communication?

    -   How does being aware of your own comfort zone help you to communicate in a different way?

    -   In what way does the Win by Losing method and communicating in a way which is consistent with the five Relationship Enablers differ from your current approach to communicating with your partner?

2. What action have you taken to expand your comfort zone?

    -   Have you completed the exercise provided in this chapter? How did you feel at first? In what way did this change over the five days?

    -   How much of the Win by Losing method have you applied to the way you communicate in your relationship?

    -   What about the Relationship Enablers? Have your included them in the way you communicate too? If so, write down three examples. If you can, discuss these with your partner. Does she agree?

What's Next?

In the next chapter we will provide more detail about putting *Win by Losing* into practice. As this is the last chapter, it ties the whole book together and enables you to prepare your action plan.

CHAPTER 10

Don't just sit there: How to put Win by Losing into Practice

Well done is better than well said.

BENJAMIN FRANKLIN, A FOUNDING
FATHER OF THE UNITED STATES

Why read this chapter? What's in it for you?

In this chapter we will cover:

- ► Time to act: What taking action means in the context of Win by Losing;

- ► Lifestyle choice: What this means in practice;

- ► Your world: How we create our own reality;

- ► Great expectations: Expecting a little too much;

- ► Creating options: There's always a positive future;

- ► Staying together: How to avoid relationship drift;

- ► Putting it all together: Your 90-day action plan;

- ► Key Points;

- ► Questions and Answers;

- ► Multiple Choice;

▶ Take Action.

Let's make a start: Introduction

It's time to act!

As explained in previous chapters, most people have a built-in understanding and appreciation of fairness. We want to remind you that Ground rules must be fair and reasonable – they should never be used as an excuse to control your partner.

Ground rules must never force your partner to do something she doesn't want to do. It's unfair, unreasonable and will fill your partner's Sink of Negativity.

Applying the Win by Losing method and communicating in a way which is consistent with the five Relationship Enablers keeps the level of friction between you to a minimum. Focusing on your ground rules means you can put all your Emotional Energy into enforcing those aspects of your life and your relationship which are important to you. Keep them to a practical minimum so you can win those arguments when your ground rules need to be enforced.

Be clear and consistent. Take responsibility for your communication and remember not to plant unnecessary negative words in your partner's complex web of emotions, which concurrently operate on so many different levels.

The fact is that most of the many hours we spend with our partners are when we are going about our daily lives. Although these are not special times, they can be happy when the relationship works for both of you.

Winning, in the context of this book, is simply having a happy relationship, one where you look forward to the times you spend with your partner. They don't need to be special times, but every time is a happy time.

However, this is *not* therapeutic intervention. We are not suggesting the content of this book is used as a treatment to solve a problem. Moreover, we don't suggest writing down anything concerned with making complicated agreements with each other. If you feel a list of agreed points is needed, it needs to be facilitated by a professional. Unless you receive the type of support needed, putting words on a piece of paper will do nothing to change the way you communicate.

If, however, you find that your partner is not interested in improving your relationship, if she doesn't have the same positive intent as you, then it's time to ask yourself why you are together. Any relationship, especially an intimate one, should enhance your life and not leave you feeling upset, stressed, miserable, and alone.

Keeping calm: Discuss your Relationship Enablers

It is often said that knowledge is power. Understanding the five Relationship Enablers will empower you to take the necessary action, by talking with your partner in a planned, calm, and understanding manner, thereby enabling you both to adapt your communication and subsequent behavior accordingly.

We want to emphasize the importance of having this type of discussion in a composed and understanding manner. Most of us tackle relationship issues at a time when the issue at hand matters to us the most—and that's normally in the middle of an argument. However, we very much doubt that positive and long-lasting change will be agreed during an argument.

Focus on the causes rather than the symptoms.

A new way to live your life: Lifestyle choice

If matters are already so bad that the negativity can no longer flow away from the Sink of Negativity, the Win by Losing method alone will not solve your problems—that's what relationship counselors are paid to do. They can effectively take a bucket and remove that negative energy by scooping it out from the top, so it falls below the critical point of no return.

This book is about adopting a lifestyle choice in the way you communicate and interact with your partner. By keeping to this approach, you will avoid unnecessary arguments and wasteful friction between you and replace it with happier and more intimate times together.

The importance of preserving your Emotional Energy cannot be overstated. This must be saved for, and invested in, enforcing your ground rules. Don't go spoiling things by having unnecessary arguments which you will probably lose anyway. It's a long-term commitment which requires determination and focus.

Compatibility: You always have a choice

If the benefits enjoyed by adopting the Winning by Losing method still don't leave you with a happy relationship, still leave you feeling unhappy, or if you find your partner is never satisfied with the relationship no matter what, then perhaps she's not the right person for you.

Being in a relationship is ultimately a choice. Yes, where children are involved, this makes the decision to leave far more complicated and difficult. Even so if she is not the right person for you, then action needs to be taken to put yourself in a position to break free. After all, we have already established the fact that you won't be able to change her, just as she is unable to change you.

Being in a relationship is ultimately a choice.

No more fighting: Teamwork

If you work together as a team and support each other in the mundane daily routine which, let's be honest, is a great part of how we spend our lives, then you will be well prepared to work as a team when life gets tough and throws curve balls. That happens to all of us.

If you don't act as a team when life is easy, dealing with the day-to-day challenges, then don't be surprised when you find the relationship can't handle it when life gets difficult. Establish a team approach when life is good, in order to support each other effectively when it gets difficult—and that includes if, or when, you have kids.

Do you create your world? Your reality

Although not wanting to become philosophical in a book for men about relationships and communication, it does need to be appreciated that men and women create their own reality where relationships are concerned.

What do we mean by this? We decide our ground rules and what's most important to us. We attract the type of person we date by the way we behave, what we wear, and where we choose to go in order to meet someone. We decide who to date; and choose with whom we form intimate relationships. Unless you are in an arranged marriage, nobody else does this for us.

However, the creation of our own reality goes further than this. Have you noticed how funny things seem to happen to the same people, and yet everything seems to go wrong for others? Or how some people always seem to be unlucky in everything they do, whereas dramatic things seem to happen to others? How is it that some people are able to make a fortune and, even if they lose it, make their fortune again? Why is this the case?

Another way of asking this same question is, "Why do the same things happen to the same people?" There is only one constant and that's the people in question. This can only mean that these people create their own reality. We all do.

*The inescapable truth here is that if you want your life in terms of intimate relationships to change, then the first consideration, **the most important person who needs to change, is you**.*

You need to change your ground rules, your communication, your behavior, and decide what's most important to you about your relationship. We are not saying this is easy, but we are saying that **change can only start with you**.

A university professor went to visit a famous Zen master. While the master quietly served tea, the professor talked in great detail about Zen. The master poured the visitor's cup to the brim, and then kept pouring. The professor watched the overflowing cup until he could no longer restrain himself.

"It's full! No more will go in!" the professor blurted.

"This is you," the master replied. "How can I show you Zen unless you first empty your cup?" (http://truecenterpublishing.com/zen-story/emptycup.html)

Your Sink of Negativity doesn't care about your childhood; it has no interest in what's happened in your life over the years. It doesn't care about whether you grew up in poverty or luxury. There's no favoritism where your religion or ethnicity is concerned. When negativity outweighs positivity in your relationship for long enough, your relationship will come to an unhappy end. When positivity outweighs negativity, you empty the Sink of Negativity and enjoy the fruits of a happy relationship.

It's all about the way you think and communicate where your relationship is concerned; about taking personal responsibility for your communication and, of course, your behavior.

Where Win by Losing is concerned you are responsible for your communication. You are responsible for your actions. There's no room for blaming anyone else, complaining about your childhood or the way life has treated you. It starts and ends with *you*.

Change from within yourself will lead to change in your relationship. Changes that only you can make to how you communicate are far more powerful than fruitless attempts to change your partner. **Your partner will not, cannot, change for you, just as you can't change for her.**

Changing yourself is something you can most certainly do whenever you like. You can start right now. What's stopping you, other than you? Win by Losing. The choice is yours.

Great expectations: Expecting a little too much

Unfortunately, many of us expect too much from ourselves and our partners, whether married or not. We expect ourselves to look perfect and for our lives to be perfect too. Nobody's life is perfect. That's just the way life is.

Increasingly, fueled by the illusion of perfection in mass and social media, with the associated Fear of Missing Out (FOMO), we create impossible expectations from our lives and our relationships. Those who expect less from themselves and those around them live happier lives as their day-to-day experiences live up to their more realistic expectations.

Many of us expect too much from our ourselves and our partners.

Having unnecessarily high expectations inevitably leads to disappointment. What does this mean for you? Possibly nothing… or possibly your unreasonably high expectations are preventing you from finding happiness.

Granted, more realistic expectations won't necessarily make you happy, but they will reduce the chances of feeling disappointed and unhappy.

> He lets all things come and go
>
> effortlessly, without desire.
>
> He never expects results;
>
> thus he is never disappointed.

LAO TZU, TAO TE CHING, CHAPTER 55

We aren't saying you should have no expectations in your relationship. Instead, you need to navigate between having no expectations at all and unrealistic expectations. The ideal is to land somewhere in the middle.

There are always options: When nothing works

Returning to Win by Losing, being in a relationship with your partner is like looking after a vintage car. It takes time, effort, and patience by both of you. To expect a relationship to just *work out* is unrealistic. Equally, there is the possibility that the ideas contained in this book will not work in your relationship.

Keep your ground rules simple and employ the method of Win by Losing for a happy relationship. That's how it is supposed to work… except for when it doesn't. For instance:

- when no ground rule is regarded as reasonable and is attacked at every opportunity;

- when your partner competes with you no matter what;

- when she only plays tennis and rowing is out of the question.

Some women—and men—behave in this way and, given the opportunity, treat their partner as a doormat. There is no point trying to change them as we have already established that approach will not work.

Furthermore, in this context, finding something to change in yourself will be ineffective. Under these circumstances, a different approach is needed.

In a modern, liberal democracy, being in a relationship isn't mandatory.

If you find that your partner actively works against you no matter what you do, and if no ground rules are permitted, you need to take action. You need to sit down and talk to her about it, or you may decide to seek professional help from a counselor. This book is certainly no substitute for what can be achieved by an experienced counselor when you both are willing to pursue this course of action. However, even counselors can't work miracles.

Applying the Win by Losing method and communicating in a way which is consistent with the five Relationship Enablers serves to empower men by enabling them to communicate with their partners more effectively, thereby promoting a happy relationship.

Clearly, for a man to be happy in a relationship he needs to have his own identity and his ground rules upheld. If your partner can't do that, then she probably doesn't respect you. It's that lack of respect that can potentially turn you into a doormat and nobody should have to put up with nonsense like that.

Don't assume that because she loves you (or appears to), she respects you. These are two different dimensions of a relationship and they are independent of each other. It's possible to be respected but not loved, so why not loved but not respected?

Win by Losing enables men to communicate with their partners more effectively, thereby promoting a happy relationship.

Love without respect is a dangerous combination. Where nothing seems to work, you must have the courage to face the option of leaving her. This is easier said than done, we appreciate that. However, if you feel your relationship is toxic, the way you communicate with each other nasty, the water level in your sink high, then Win by Losing becomes Win by *Leaving*. Just like Win by Losing, the choice is yours.

> The wrong person makes you beg for attention, affection, love and commitment. The right person gives you these things because they love you.
>
> SONYA PARKER, AUTHOR

Your 90-day Action Plan

At this point you have either:

1. Been applying the *Take Action* sections at the end of every chapter and have already started to notice a genuine improvement to the way you communicate, and are therefore starting to achieve the results you want.

2. Read the book, or the chapters which most interested you, but have yet to apply any of the content to your relationship.

If you fall under the second category, the 90-day action plan is especially for you.

How do you put what we have covered in this book into practice? You can choose a chapter, or specific subtopics from one or more chapters, and apply this content to the way you communicate with your partner.

It's likely one or more of the Relationship Enablers, for example, resonate with you more than others, or you identify more closely with some of the subtopics. In that case, take what you feel will make the biggest difference and adopt that approach.

It may be that you are single at the moment and will use some of our suggestions one day in the future. Keep our book handy: We're sure you will find the content helpful at the right time for you.

Alternatively, you may prefer to follow our 90-day action plan. We can't make this plan for you; it's your relationship and your plan must be relevant to your circumstances. However, we can give you a list of questions to consider (see Appendix 1), formed as a collation of all the "Take Action" sections at the end of every chapter.

So, how does it work?

- You select no more than two to five of these questions and use your answers as a basis for the action you will take over the next thirty days. Consider why you have selected those particular questions and what outcome you seek.

- Be clear in your mind how communication between you and your partner will change as a consequence of your action. A pragmatic approach is much more likely to be effective – you need to be realistic!

- When the desired change has taken place, revisit the 90-day action plan list of questions and undertake the same process. Keep with this approach and you will have completed at least nine action points in 90 days. That will make a considerable difference to the way you communicate with your partner and therefore how you both experience the time you spend together.

Win by Losing is a lifestyle choice, meaning that it's a way of living your life every day where your intimate relationship is concerned.

Completing your 90-day action plan is just the springboard to get you started. Remain focused and you will be able to maintain this approach to the way you communicate with your partner and enjoy the long-term benefits Win by Losing provides.

Staying together: Avoiding relationship drift

It's not uncommon to hear, "I don't know why but we just drifted apart over the years." We know why. It's because the relationship was in neutral and nobody did anything about it. It's like leaving an airplane hurtling along at 550 miles per hour with nobody at the controls. If left for long enough, the airplane will crash—not unlike a relationship, in which both parties take each other and their relationship for granted.

When running a car, you have a service once a year. The tires need to be monitored and changed when they are worn, the oil checked, and the wiper fluid refilled when it is empty. You don't expect to get into your car every morning and for it to work perfectly for months or years on end without looking after it. But that's exactly how most of us treat our relationships.

Your 90-day plan shouldn't be a one-off. We recommend either revisiting your plan or creating new one by going through the questions in Appendix 1: Your 90-Day Action Plan every year, to ensure your relationship remains on track. This prevents unnecessary and entirely preventable relationship drift.

Servicing your car is expensive. An annual relationship review, on the other hand, is free.

Talk about this with your partner. If there are some difficult conversations to have then you need to have them. The alternative is for your Sinks of Negativity to slowly fill and for the two of you to drift apart. It doesn't need to be this way. Make sure you are in the driving seat where your relationship is concerned. Win by Losing. The choice is yours.

Putting it all together: "Happy Choice" mnemonic

Throughout this book we have stressed the importance of your always having a choice in order to achieve happiness in your relationship. The following mnemonic serves to summarize some of our key points:

- **H**: *Healthy and effective communication* is fundamental to a happy relationship.

- **A**: *Actively* work to maintain honest, clear and effective channels of communication, by keeping the amount of negativity in your Sink of Negativity to a minimum.

- **P**: *Practicing active listening* will develop this important skill. This is far more important to women that most men realize.

- **P**: *Pillars* of the Win by Losing model—the Relationship Enablers—are crucial. They form the basis upon which our happiness rests.

- **Y**: *Yearly relationship reviews* are free, don't need to take long, and enable you to maintain a happy relationship.

- **C**: *Comfort zones* apply to all of us. They are part of the human condition.

- **H**: *Hope leads to hopelessness.* Don't hope, act, and make positive changes to the way you communicate.

- **O**: *Organize your time* so you spend enough quality time with your partner.

- **I**: *Incorporate* the sections of this book which resonate with you the most. Then move on to the other sections and incorporate them too. The more action you take, the better your relationship will become.

- **C**: *Change comes from within you.* Don't try to change your partner as this approach will fail.

- **E:** *Everyone can benefit from the Win by Losing method* supported by communicating in a way which is consistent with the Relationship Enablers. That includes you too!

No time like the present: Over to you

Unless you have already made a start, either take a look at Appendix 1 and develop your 90-Day Action Plan, or go back to the chapters which interested you most, and apply those exercises and questions to your relationship.

A Happy Relationship = A Happy You. What's more important than that?

Whatever route you take, remember change takes time and determination. It doesn't matter if your 90-day action plan takes more or less time than this. Any change, no matter how minor, is a step in the right direction. Change can be a slow, time-consuming, and challenging process. Don't expect too much from yourself or your partner and celebrate every step in the right direction.

Rome wasn't built-in a day, but they were laying bricks every hour

JAMES CLEAR, PLAYWRIGHT

Key points diary

If you find there's a lot to do from your 90-day action plan, keeping a personal diary for between two to four weeks can prove useful. Rather than record everything that happens each day, just keep a record of progress against your action points and how they impact on how you communicate with your partner. It will enable you to track your progress and develop an understanding of which topics are the most important for you.

Consider expanding your personal diary to include answers to some of these statements:

- My ground rules are…

- My partner's ground rules are…

- I felt good about our relationship today because…

- We had an argument today about…

- I Won by Losing today by…

- I Listened with intent today when…

- I spent quality time with my partner today by…

- I showed affection toward my partner today when I/we …

- I was assertive rather than aggressive today when…

- I didn't add to my partner's web of negative emotions unnecessarily today by…

- I ensured I wasn't treated like a doormat today when…

- I tackled an issue identified in my 90-day action plan today by…

- I interpreted what my partner said to me correctly today when…

- I told my partner what was on my mind today, rather than complain about her to someone else when…

- I noticed how a small change in my communication had a positive impact on my relationship today when…

- I changed a potential game of tennis against my partner today into rowing together by…

- I put down my smartphone today and focused entirely on my partner when…

Writing your thoughts down puts them into perspective and enables you to make comparisons when you revisit them in the future.

Key Points

1. It's important to spend time reading and thinking about communication in your relationship. However, *nothing will change until you take action.*

2. In this book "winning" is all about having a happy relationship, one in which you look forward to the times you spend with your partner.

3. Expecting too much inevitably leads to disappointment. Don't expect so much from yourself or your relationship. Nobody is perfect and any relationship is just a bonding of two imperfect people.

4. Win by Losing does not operate alone as it is underpinned by the five Relationship Enablers needed for this approach to be effective and to keep levels of unnecessary friction to a minimum. This approach empowers you to communicate in a more effective way to achieve the results you seek.

5. Win by Losing enables you to communicate with your partner more effectively, thereby promoting a happy relationship. If none of the ideas in this book work, if you have tried professional counseling and are still unhappy, you are probably in a relationship with the wrong person. This is when Win by Losing becomes Win by *Leaving.*

Questions and Answers

Q: What is *Win by Losing*?

A: Win by Losing is a way to handle your intimate relationship that focuses on knowing when to choose your battles and having a better understanding how to communicate effectively with the woman in your life. This enables both you and your partner to have a happy, meaningful and satisfying relationship.

This is achieved by:

- Understanding what you want and hold dear in your relationship;

- Discussing and understanding how to solve problems together;

- Recognizing the cost of arguments and doing something about it;

- Developing constructive direct communication;

- Making sure that what you hear is what she said;

- Identifying how to react in unfamiliar situations.

It's a simple way of communicating which works in conjunction with five Relationship Enablers as follows:

1. **I won't back down: Enforce your ground rules** (Chapter 4): Ground Rules are the most important things to you in your life and relationship. Enforcing them ensures they stay in place.

2. **Make every conversation matter: Listening with Intent** (Chapter 5): A way of listening to your partner which encourages effective communication.

3. **We're in this together: Common purpose** (Chapter 6): Understanding why you are in a relationship together to ensure you both achieve the outcomes you desire.

4. **Just accept it: Acceptance of what we can and cannot change** (Chapter 7): No matter how much you love your partner, you can't change her. Change can only come from within you.

5. **Say what you mean: Straight talking** (Chapter 8): Saying what's really on your mind in a calm and constructive manner.

Q: All the magazines I read show wealthy, beautiful people marrying other wealthy, beautiful people. Their relationships and lives are perfect. Shouldn't my relationship be the same?

A: Given the rate of divorce and separation among famous people, you should ask yourself if their relationships really are that perfect. Don't fall for the professional Public Relations machine. They are just people like the rest of us and their relationships are also affected by life's pressures. There is no such thing as perfection where two human beings are concerned. Don't expect so much from yourself and your partner.

Q: I have tried everything with my partner, but she just isn't interested in communicating in a better way. She's just nasty to me. What can I do?

A: If you really have tried the ideas set out in this book and your partner is continuing to behave in a negative way toward you, go to a professional counselor. If that doesn't work, it's time to leave her and move on. Whether or not you are married, it's a relationship not a prison.

Q: Must there be issues in our relationship to benefit from the Win by Losing method?

A: Not at all. You can use the ideas contained throughout this book to make a good relationship even better.

Q: What do you mean by a "lifestyle choice"?

A: Win by Losing is a way of communicating with your partner. It's not something which springs into action when there is an issue between you, and is forgotten about when things go well. It's a way to live your life where your relationship is concerned. That makes it a lifestyle choice.

Q: What's relationship drift?

A: It's when the two of you unintentionally start to drift apart. This isn't uncommon and can be prevented by undertaking annual relationship reviews. Spend a little time answering the questions in Appendix 1: Your 90-Day Action Plan. It doesn't cost anything and will make the world of difference.

Q: Why do I need a 90-day action plan?

A: You need to put the ideas and suggestions contained in this book into action and this is an effective way of doing so.

Multiple Choice

1. For the Win by Losing method to be effective you need to:

    a. Read the book over and over again and hope something changes.

    b. Apply the ideas contained in this book to the way you communicate in your relationship.

    c. Give a copy of this book to your partner and ask her to tell you where she is going wrong.

    d. Send copies of this book to your partner's best friends and her parents. They'll know what to do.

2. You need to preserve your Emotional Energy by adopting the Win by Losing method because:

    a. Most women have larger Emotional Energy batteries than men and their charge-up times are shorter. By preserving your Emotional Energy, you are able to ensure your ground rules are enforced successfully. The alternative is to waste your Emotional Energy on matters which are less important.

    b. It's fun to use it all up by having regular and unnecessary arguments.

    c. You can sell any excess Emotional Energy on eBay and make a profit from it.

    d. Emotional Energy of this type is useful when negotiating salary increases at work.

3. You always fall in love with difficult women because:

    a. You keep taking your best friend's advice. It's all his fault.

    b. Your parents create your reality and it's all their fault.

    c.   You like it when your partner keeps you on your toes.

    d.   You create your own reality, attract that type of woman, and choose to have a relationship with them.

4.   All intimate relationships, no matter how strong, are at risk of relationship drift. The best way of ensuring this doesn't happen is:

    a.   Tell your partner regularly not to drift away from you.

    b.   Buy flowers for your partner every week.

    c.   Revisit the questions in Appendix 1: Your 90-day Action Plan on at least an annual basis.

    d.   Marry your partner and have children.

5.   You don't want to miss out. Your relationship should be perfect because:

    a.   You are in love and that means you are two perfect human beings coming together in happiness and harmony.

    b.   Everyone else on social media is happy, so you should be too.

    c.   You have almost finished reading this book. Improving the way you communicate with your partner will create the perfect relationship where you never argue.

    d.   Relationships *should* be perfect. In real life though, nobody is perfect and relationships certainly aren't perfect either. Social media has fueled unrealistically high expectations of you and your partner. Nothing in life is perfect.

6.   You should consider ending your relationship when:

    a.   You have worked hard to communicate in a way which is consistent with the five Relationship Enablers and your communication has changed as a consequence. But no matter how hard you try, she has no interest in "you." Her only interest is getting her own way. You have tried couples therapy but that didn't work either.

b. Your partner starts talking about your future and having a family. It all sounds too serious for your liking.

c. You've tried, in a halfhearted sort of way, to apply a few of the ideas contained in this book. They didn't work and your partner continues to be annoyed with you about pretty much everything you do.

d. Your partner finished reading this book and thought it was a great work of fiction.

Take Action

Take some time to answer and act upon these questions.

1. Is adopting the ideas contained in this book part of your new relationship communication lifestyle?

    - Do you only think about Win by Losing when things become difficult between you?

    - Does your Sink of Negativity have to be relatively full in order for you to take action in a positive way?

    - How will you incorporate what has been covered in this book into the way you communicate with your partner every day? Will you act upon your answers from the "Take Action" sections at the end of every chapter? How about working through your 90-day action plan? Considered keeping a diary of your successes? Possibly a combination of these?

2. How do you ensure your Emotional Energy is preserved for when you really need it?

    - Write down what preserving your Emotional Energy means to you.

    - Provide three examples of achieving a "win" by adopting the Win by Losing method.

- Nobody's perfect. We are sure you have wasted some of your Emotional Energy arguing about something not associated with a ground rule. Write down an example and how this could have been handled in a different way.

3. Do you blame everyone around you every time things don't go your way?

    - What's the one constant factor in your life?

    - When something happens which doesn't work out well for you, write down what you will do differently the next time something like this happens again.

4. What action are you taking to avoid relationship drift?

    - Have you thought about having a conversation with your partner about this, but not had the time or found the right moment? Have you come up against your comfort zone?

    - Have you carried out an Annual Review of your relationship with your partner? If not, why not? Found time to watch television, use your smartphone, or go to the gym instead?

5. Have you yet to take any action and don't know where to start with you 90-day action plan?

    - Keeping a key points diary for two to four weeks will help you to identify which action to prioritize.

    - Is communicating in a different way outside your comfort zone? If so, complete the comfort zone exercise in Chapter 9: Comfort Zones (see "Take Action").

AFTERWORD

We hope you have enjoyed reading this book and putting the content into practice. Please send us an email to authors@WinByLosingBook.com as we would appreciate your feedback on how the content of this book has worked for you. This book is all about making a positive difference and we want to hear how it's made a difference to you and your partner.

Interested in more information? Check out our website www.WinByLosingBook.com or our Facebook page, Win by Losing Book, for further details.

Note: Our email, website, and Facebook page are Win by Losing Book.

APPENDIX 1: YOUR 90-DAY ACTION PLAN

The questions listed below comprise all of the questions available in the "Take action" sections at the end of every chapter.

If you decide to create a 90-day action plan, consider any of the questions listed below, which are categorized by topic, and based on these questions, decide upon your action points. We recommend the following steps:

1. Focus on no more than 3–5 action points from within your 90-day action plan, in the first 30 days. We assume this will take about 30 days but it may take longer. When you feel these have been addressed, revisit the entire list below and address 3–5 more action points, which you can develop from any of the questions listed below.

2. Maintain this approach and you will complete at least 9 action points in 90 days. That will make a considerable difference to the way you communicate with your partner and therefore to how you both experience the time you spend together.

Win by Losing is a lifestyle choice, meaning that it's a way of living your life every day where your relationship is concerned. Completing your 90-day action plan is just the springboard to get you started. Maintain this approach and enjoy the long-term benefits the Win by Losing method provides.

Chapter: 1 – Introduction

1. What do you want from your relationship? What makes you happy?

   - Write down a list of 3–5 things that you want from your relationship. Keep it simple because overcomplicating it sets you up for failure.

   - Put your list away and look at it in a few days' time. Are you sure these things will make you happy in your relationship? It's worth giving this some thought and ensuring the list is right for you.

   - How many of your points are being met fully right now? If some, or all, aren't being met, read on!

2. What is the difference between active and passive reading? What will you do to ensure you read actively?

   - Answer each of the questions in the Q&A section before checking your understanding is correct?

   - Complete the Multiple Choice section (answers are available in Appendix 2)?

   - Write down your responses to the 'Take Action' section at the end of every chapter?

   - Carry out all or some of our exercises?

   - Utilize the 90-day action plan available in Appendix 1?

   - A combination of these things?

3. There is no best time to read this book. What are your circumstances right now?

   - If you are in a difficult relationship which you would like to improve, what makes the relationship difficult? How could the way you communicate together change in order for you to be happy?

- If you are in a happy relationship which you feel could be even better, what needs to change?

- If you are single, what are you looking for in your next relationship? And how open are you to handling your communication differently next time?

4. What does "intimacy" mean to you?

- This term is open to interpretation, but what does it mean to you right now?

- Is your relationship at the level of intimacy which works best for you? If not, you need to read the rest of this book before addressing this issue.

5. Why is Win by Losing a lifestyle choice?

- If you have read this chapter, you will know the answer!

- Are you open to the idea of adopting a new approach to communicating with your partner? If yes, keep reading in an active way.

Chapter: 2 – What is Win by Losing?

1. Write down three examples where you lost an argument with your partner because you simply ran out of Emotional Energy.

- All men have plenty of examples so don't kid yourself that you have none!

- Given what we have covered in this chapter, how could you have handled those situations differently? Would the long-term outcome have been any different?

2. How might you choose your battles more wisely in the future?

- What does that mean about those arguments which, when you stop to think about it, were about things that weren't important to you?

- How will this approach impact your relationship right now?

3. What are your ground rules?

   - Make a list of those things which matter the most to you in your relationship and life. These are the things worth arguing about!

   - Have you ever argued about issues which are *not* on your list? Why? How did the argument work out? Was it worth it?

4. Are you treated like a doormat?

   - If yes, why do you think that is the case? Is there mutual respect in your relationship?

   - What simple ground rules could you put in place to stop this from happening in the future?

   - How will you communicate your ground rules to your partner? Read about the Relationship Enablers (Chapters 3–8) before having this type of conversation.

5. If you have had an unhappy breakup in the past, why did your Sink of Negativity overflow?

   - Provide three examples where negativity was added to the sink.

   - Given what you know about the Win by Losing method, how could this have been handled differently?

6. Positive communication and experiences together reduce the water level in your Sink of Negativity.

   - Make a list of between three and six actions you can take over the next week to reduce the water level in your relationship's Sink of Negativity.

   - Review the list in a week's time. Did you complete all your actions? If so, in what way has this affected the way the two of you communicate? If not, why not? And what will you do differently in future?

7. Given what you now know about Emotional Energy, how might you handle friction or an argument in the future?

    •   Thinking about the disagreements and arguments you have with your partner; which are worth having? What about the others?

    •   Which disagreements and arguments are better handled by adopting the Win by Losing method?

    •   How would adopting the Win by Losing method change the ultimate outcome of your arguments?

    •   List the advantages and disadvantages to you of adopting the Win by Losing method.

8. Over the next week or two, write down each time you saved your Emotional Energy and when you needed to use it.

    •   Describe how you were better able to win when you had preserved your Emotional Energy for when it was really needed.

    •   If you were unable to preserve your Emotional Energy, were you really adopting the Win by Losing method, and only arguing to enforce your ground rules? See Chapter 4 for more information and detail on ground rules.

    •   How has adopting the Win by Losing method changed the way you communicate with your partner? How has it changed the way your partner communicates with you? What has been the effect on your Sink of Negativity?

    •   All change takes time and, if it's a new approach, adopting the Win by Losing method will also take time to become second nature to you. It will also take time for your partner to adjust to your new way of communicating. What have you learned about applying the Win by Losing method to the way you communicate every day? What changes, if any, have you experienced as a result of adopting this approach? What further changes would you like to achieve? How do you plan to achieve these further changes?

Chapter: 3 – Relationship Enablers: An introduction

1. Describe the first few months of your current or previous relationships. Typically, over this time you started off with no internal or external pressures and they slowly built over time.

    - What were the first internal and external pressures which you can recall?

    - How did the relationship change as time went on? Where these changes sudden or did they creep up on you?

    - What effect did these changes have on your relationship and, most importantly, how you communicated? With the power of hindsight and what you have covered so far in this book, how could you have handled these changes in a different way?

2. Write down a list of internal and external pressures on your relationship. An awareness of these is needed if you are to tackle them in a constructive way.

    - If you are single, choose a previous relationship.

    - Ask your partner to write down what she sees as the internal and external pressures on the relationship.

    - Spend a little time comparing your lists. What's similar? What's different?

    - Which pressures are just a part of life and which are self-imposed? Can any of them be removed by the two of you communicating and working together in a better way?

3. Think about and write down common arguments you have with your partner.

   • Are there any underlying themes or issues to these arguments, which act as fuel to keep these arguments reoccurring? Keep those themes in mind when reading the Relationship Enablers in Chapters 4 – 8.

   • If the underlying issues are difficult to determine, keep a diary of your arguments and, in about two weeks, review your diary. The themes should become clear.

Chapter: 4 – I won't back down: Enforce your Ground Rules

1. Write down your ground rules.

   • Are they fair, reasonable, simple to understand, and few in number?

   • Have you discussed your ground rules with anyone before?

   • What changes, if any, need to be made to the way you communicate in your relationship so these ground rules are respected by your partner?

2. How well do you enforce your ground rules?

   • Do you preserve all your Emotional Energy for the enforcement of your ground rules?

   • When you do have to enforce your ground rules, do you remind your partner of what they are and explain why they are important to you? People rarely remember and act upon what we say to them when we shout and blame!

3. If your partner is to respect your ground rules, how do you respect hers? Respect is a two-way street and you need to look both ways.

   • What are your partner's ground rules?

- Explain to your partner what ground rules are and ask her to think about hers. The starting point is to ask, "What's most important to you about our relationship and in your life right now?" If the answer isn't a ground rule, ask, "What's important to you about that?" You may need to ask the latter question a number of times to discover each of her ground rules. Give your partner some time to think about her ground rules. She probably hasn't thought about this before.

- When you know your partner's ground rules, how will you respect them?

- Write down examples when you have respected your partner's ground rules.

- Write down examples when you did not respect your partner's ground rules and describe what happened. Be honest with yourself.

4. How does your partner enforce her ground rules?

- If you know your partner's ground rules, does she still have to enforce them? If so, why?

- Have you ever broken one of your partner's ground rules because she broke one of yours? What was the outcome of this way of communicating? Did it lower the Sink of Negativity and leave you both happy and content? If you feel it's relevant, discuss a better way of communicating.

5. Does your partner know your ground rules?

- Have you talked about your ground rules in a calm and constructive way?

- Have you listened to her concerns and ensured your ground rules are fair, reasonable and few in number? You shouldn't have a never-ending wish list!

- Does your partner respect your ground rules? If not, why not? Do you respect hers?

6. How does Win by Losing empower you to enforce your ground rules?

    - How much Emotional Energy do you have compared to your partner? Life's tough—be honest.

    - Describe how having a lower water level in the Sink of Negativity, fewer disagreements and less friction/stress between you affect the way you communicate together.

    - In what way are you better able to enforce your ground rules when adopting the Win by Losing method?

7. If one of your ground rules has changed, have you informed your partner?

    - Have you thought through why your ground rule has changed and how this will affect your partner?

    - If you were on the receiving end of your ground rule change, what questions and concerns might you have?

    - When is the best time to raise your change of ground rule with your partner? Probably not, for example, after she's had a long and challenging day at work.

8. What's the difference between playing tennis against each other and rowing together?

    - How do you communicate with your partner? Do you play tennis or row together? Write down examples of both.

    - If you play tennis against each other, why is this the case? Does it have to be this way? Adopting the Win by Losing method will lower the Sink of Negativity which, in turn, creates the context for rowing together. Be patient as change takes time.

- Write down examples of when you rowed together rather than played tennis against each other. Talk to your partner about this and acknowledge these successes together.

9. If you must play tennis in order to enforce your ground rules, do you win?

    - If not, is your list of ground rules sufficiently short? Have you adopted the Win by Losing method for everything else?

10. Is there a healthy balance of power between you?

    - Do you have control over your partner? Does she have control over you?

    - Are you able to describe each other's ground rules?

    - Do you understand and respect each other's ground rules in a consistent manner? Have you ever talked about this with your partner?

Chapter: 5 – Make every conversation matter: Listening with Intent

Listen, Focus, Say

Put Listening with Intent into practice by remembering three words: Listen, Focus, Say:

- *Listen* to what your partner is saying;

- *Focus* on her words (not the voice inside your head that's wondering what's for dinner); and

- *Say* a brief summary of what she has said back to your partner.

Exercise: Conversation Feedback

With a friend or your partner ask them to have a conversation with you and share five things about themselves which you may not know. Then provide them with a summary of what they have just said to you.

They then tell you five more things and you repeat those back to them too. They shouldn't just list these for you. That would be too easy and not how conversations normally work. You should be the one asking questions to gain this information.

Next, your friend or partner should tell you about what's been happening in their lives over the last week or so. It doesn't need to be exciting or interesting events, just what's been happening. Listen for 3–5 minutes and summarize this back to them. It's not as easy as it sounds. Variations include: asking your friend or partner about their holiday, childhood, interests, or hobbies. There are always opportunities to practice listening with intent.

Repeat these exercises weekly and you will find your ability to listen with intent quickly improves over time. Whatever happens, and however long it takes to master this Relationship Enabler, your efforts will not go unrewarded.

Listening with intent ensures the time you spend together is seen as quality time by your partner. It will also reduce the instances of misunderstanding and, in time, will make for an easier way of communicating.

By adopting the Win by Losing method, enforcing your clearly communicated ground rules, respecting your partner's ground rules and listening with intent, you will soon notice a transformation in your relationship.

Exercise: Partner Feedback

The way men and women communicate with each other differs quite considerably. Over the next week or so we recommend spending time listening when women talk to each other. You will notice how they can be far more interactive and communicative than men. It's rare for a woman to reply with "Hmm. Okay," so you should avoid it too.

As an exercise, adopt the approach of summarizing back briefly what you hear to your partner. We are certain that you will be surprised how much your communication will improve. Listening with intent is an important Relationship Enabler as it ensures your partner feels that you listen to what she has to say. It also ensures you really *do* listen to what she has says as it's simply not possible to listen in this way and fail to absorb what is being said.

Take some time to answer these questions.

1. Write down what quality time with your partner means to you.

    - Your interpretation of quality time may be different from that of your partner. What does it mean to her? How do you know? Have you asked?

    - Based on **your** interpretation of quality time, give examples of how, when, and where you and your partner have spent quality time together over the past three months.

    - Based on **your partner's** interpretation of quality time, ask her to give examples of how, when, and where you and her have spent quality time together over the past three months.

    - Do you spend enough quality time together, based on **both** your interpretations on what constitutes quality time? If yes, that's great. If not, what changes are needed? Does your partner agree?

    - Where changes are needed to the amount or type of quality time you spend together, agree a date and time for the two of you to review whether these changes have taken place. If you don't, how will you know that you are spending enough quality time together – according to **both** of you?

    - Do you really listen and care about what your partner has to say?

    - Write down examples of when you have Listened with Intent over the past two weeks.

- Show your examples to your partner. Does she agree with you? If not, why not?

- Listening with intent takes time and practice. Over the next two weeks, write down when you have listened in this way, and describe how it affected the way you communicate with your partner. How did listening with intent affect the Sink of Negativity?

2. What women say isn't always what they mean.

   - Do you interpret what your partner says correctly?

   - How do you know? Have you checked?

3. Have you had a long day and are not in the mood to concentrate on what your partner has to say?

   - That's okay. Just be honest and tell her. Agree a time when she will update you on, for example, the day's events and anything else that's on her mind. Make sure you follow up and spend some quality time with her.

   - Write down what happens when you adopt this approach to the way you communicate.

   - Are there ever times when your partner isn't in a frame of mind to talk with you? If so, how do you handle this? If you can ask to delay a conversation for a time that suits you better, then she can too.

Chapter: 6 – We're in this together: Common Purpose

1. Why are you in a relationship with your partner?

   - Write down what you want from your relationship. Don't worry if you're not sure. A good starting point is to ask yourself, "What's the purpose of being in a relationship with my partner? Rank each of the reasons why you are in a relationship from "1" (does not meet my needs) to "10" (meets my needs).

- It may be useful to share this with your partner. Equally it may not! That's up to you. However, if your partner doesn't know there's something wrong, she will probably assume everything is fine. Isn't that what you do?

2. Why is your partner in a relationship with you?

- What does she want out of it?

- How do you know? Have you asked her?

- If possible, share your purpose for being in your relationship and your rating of each purpose together. If this exercise is carried out in a calm and non-blaming manner, it's a great starting point to improving your relationship. However, if there are challenges in your relationship, this task is more likely to be successful if you have finished reading every chapter in this book before embarking on this exercise.

3. Are you both getting what you want from your relationship?

- Is the purpose of being together the same or different?

- Where something new is needed, identify the one change which you both agree will make the biggest difference. Focus on that one change and work together to make it happen.

- When that one thing you have agreed upon is resolved, let a few weeks go by and, if needed, identify one more. You only need to work on one thing at a time. This isn't a race!

4. Has the purpose of being in your relationship changed over time?

- Over time, our view of life and what we want from it can change. Has yours?

- If yes, what does this mean about how you communicate and spend time together? What effect has this had on your relationship? Is your partner aware of these changes? She's no mind-reader and won't know about it unless you tell her in a calm, constructive, and forward-looking, solution-focused way (that means you don't say things such as "it's all your fault").

5. Has your partner's purpose changed over time? How do you know? Have you asked her?

   - If your purpose hasn't changed over the years, don't assume the same applies to your partner.

6. How much affection, as opposed to intimacy, do you show your partner? Are you sure? Have you asked her?

   - Can you list five times over the past month when you have shown affection rather than intimacy? If you can, show this list to your partner. Does she agree these were examples of affection? If she doesn't agree (which we wouldn't find surprising) then ask her to provide you examples of what she sees as being affectionate. Whatever happens, don't react negatively to what she says to you. If you do, it may create an issue around being affectionate in your relationship and that's not a constructive way forward as it will add to the Sink of Negativity.

Chapter: 7 – Just accept it: Acceptance of what we can and cannot change

1. Do you have a "personality changes wish list" where your partner is concerned?

   - Are these changes central to your happiness in your relationship? If yes, why are you in a relationship with her?

   - If not, it's time to let that wish list go! Stop wasting your Emotional Energy trying to change her. It won't work.

2. Change can only come from within you.

- Have you accepted your partner can't change for you?

- If so, what impact did this have on your relationship?

3. Nobody is perfect. Has your partner accepted she can't change you?

    - How do you know?

4. Imagine for a moment that your partner could indeed change for you. This being the case, everyone would be able to change for the people they love.

    - Think of a former girlfriend: If you had changed for her, what sort of person would you be today?

    - Don't ask what your partner can do for you, but what you might be able to do for her.

5. Do you have an area of concern which you would like to discuss with your partner?

    - Creating the right context is key to achieving a successful outcome. This is something only you can do.

    - You can create the context needed to resolve an area of concern when you have:

    1. Adopted the Win by Losing method;

    2. Communicated and enforced your ground rules clearly;

    3. Respected your partner's ground rules;

    4. Listened with Intent *every single day*;

    5. Spent quality time together;

    6. Shown affection (not to be confused with intimacy) every day;

    7. Made ten positive remarks for every negative remark; and

    8. Accepted those things about your partner which you cannot change.

- Only then will you be well placed to have a constructive conversation about any concern you may have about your relationship. These eight points will create the positive and open context needed to have this type of conversation and enable you to achieve the outcome you seek.

- Does your partner have areas of concern too? How do you know? Have you asked and encouraged her to talk about them (preferably one at a time)?

Chapter: 8 – Say what you mean: Straight Talking

1. Are levels of intimacy too low in your relationship? Before raising this tricky issue, take the time to create a positive and constructive context in your relationship by:

    1. Adopting the Win by Losing method;

    2. Communicating and enforcing your ground rules clearly;

    3. Respecting your partner's ground rules;

    4. Listening with intent *every single day*;

    5. Spending quality time together;

    6. Showing affection (not to be confused with intimacy) every day;

    7. Making ten positive remarks for every negative remark;

    8. Accepting those things about your partner which you cannot change.

    - When the amount of negative energy in the Sinks of Negativity are low (meaning you rarely argue and enjoy each other's company), raise your concerns in a constructive and forward-looking way.

2. How many layers of thought are in your head right now?

    - How does that contrast with your partner?

- What does this mean about how you communicate with her?

3. Does your partner communicate with you in unpredictable ways?

   - Have you assumed your partner thinks the same way as you? She doesn't!

4. Have you fed your partner's spiders webs with negatively charged words recently?

   - How did that work out for you? Did it matter?

   - Were you enforcing a ground rule?

   - How could you have handled things differently?

5. Thinking about nothing?

   - What's the best way of handling this if your partner asks you about it?

6. Write down all the stars in your partner's sky.

   - Are the stars aligned? If not, what action do you need to take?

7. Have you made ten positive remarks for every negative one?

   - No? Why not? It doesn't cost anything.

   - Are you coming up against your comfort zone (see Chapter 9)?

8. Have you put your smartphone away before going to bed?

   - If there is room for improvement where intimacy is concerned, this is a good place to start.

Chapter: 9 – I am Safe: Comfort Zones

Exercise

Unless the exercise we are about to describe is something you would *normally* do, it will help you to become better aware of the feelings and thoughts you experience as you near your comfort zone. The experience will better prepare you for putting the ideas contained in this book into practice.

So, what's the exercise? All you need to do is to acknowledge the work of a service worker at least once a day for five consecutive days. You come across service workers every day: They serve you in restaurants, work in banks, call centers and offices; they keep the places you visit clean and tidy; they regularly make your lunch and clean up after you.

The next time you encounter a service worker, take an interest in them and thank them for the work they have done. Look at their name badge and use their name when thanking them. Of course, they are paid for their work, but that's not the point. You don't need to sit them down and have a fifteen-minute discussion. Just use their name and thank them for a job well done.

You may be surprised how well your good deed will be received. People tend to respond positively when we treat them with a little respect, and like fellow human beings. That's an obvious observation, but so many of us forget about it as we go about our often stressful, fast-paced, and hectic lives.

Questions

Take some time to answer and act upon these questions.

1. Is communicating in a different way, as described in this book, *within* or *outside* your comfort zone?

    - What does this mean about how you will feel when you change your communication?

    - How does being aware of your own comfort zone help you to communicate in a different way?

    - In what way does the Win by Losing method and communicating in a way which is consistent with the five Relationship Enablers differ from your current approach to communicating with your partner?

2. What action have you taken to expand your comfort zone?

   - Have you completed the exercise provided in this chapter? How did you feel at first? In what way did this change over the five days?

   - How much of the Win by Losing method have you applied to the way you communicate in your relationship?

   - What about the Relationship Enablers? Have your included them in the way you communicate too? If so, write down three examples. If you can, discuss these with your partner. Does she agree?

Chapter: 10 – Don't just sit there: How to put Win by Losing into practice

1. Is adopting the ideas contained in this book part of your new relationship communication lifestyle?

   - Do you only think about Win by Losing when things become difficult between you?

   - Does your Sink of Negativity have to be relatively full in order for you to take action in a positive way?

   - How will you incorporate what has been covered in this book into the way you communicate with your partner every day? Will you act upon your answers from the "Take Action" sections at the end of every chapter? How about working through your 90-day action plan? Considered keeping a diary of your successes? Possibly a combination of these?

2. How do you ensure your Emotional Energy is preserved for when you really need it?

   - Write down what preserving your Emotional Energy means to you.

   - Provide three examples of achieving a "win" by adopting the Win by Losing method.

- Nobody's perfect. We are sure you have wasted some of your Emotional Energy arguing about something not associated with a ground rule. Write down an example and how this could have been handled in a different way.

3. Do you blame everyone around you every time things don't go your way?

   - What's the one constant factor in your life?

   - When something happens which doesn't work out well for you, write down what you will do differently the next time something like this happens again.

4. What action are you taking to avoid relationship drift?

   - Have you thought about having a conversation with your partner about this, but not had the time or found the right moment? Have you come up against your comfort zone?

   - Have you carried out an Annual Review of your relationship with your partner? If not, why not? Found time to watch television, use your smartphone, or go to the gym instead?

5. Have you yet to take any action and don't know where to start with you 90-day action plan?

   - Keeping a key points diary for two to four weeks will help you know which action to prioritize.

   - Is communicating in a different way outside your comfort zone? If so, complete the comfort zone exercise in Chapter 9: Comfort Zones.

APPENDIX 2: MULTIPLE CHOICE ANSWERS

Chapter 1. Introduction

    1. A

    2. D

    3. C

    4. D

    5. B

Chapter 2. What is Win by Losing?

    1. B

    2. A

    3. C

    4. C

    5. B

    6. D

    7. A

Chapter 3. Relationship Enablers: An Introduction

    1. D

    2. C

    3. A

    4. B

    5. C

Chapter 4. I won't back down: Enforce your Ground Rules

1. B
2. D
3. C
4. B

Chapter 5. Make every conversation matter: Listening with Intent

1. B
2. A
3. B
4. D
5. C

Chapter 6. We're it this together: Common Purpose

1. C
2. D
3. A

Chapter 7. Just Accept It: Acceptance of what we can and cannot change

1. D
2. C
3. B
4. D
5. C

Chapter 8. Say what you mean: Straight Talking

1. D
2. C
3. C
4. A
5. B
6. D

7. C

Chapter 9. I am safe: Comfort Zones

1. B
2. A

Chapter 10. Don't just sit there: How to put *Win by Losing* into Practice

1. B
2. A
3. D
4. C
5. D
6. A